Rant Seven Rant Seven Rant Seven Rant Se

A rant is a polemic, a forceful argument and in Scots "a noisy frolic". When Norman Finkelstein was told on the Today Programme that his book was "a bit of rant", he replied that all the great polemics such as Edmund Burke's *Reflections on the Revolution in France*, Thomas Paine's *Rights of Man*, and *The Communist Manifesto* were rants, and his was just another. They are necessary voices in our national debate, but in this series we also like to keep in mind the gaiety and mischief of our noisy frolic. *Barking up the Right Tree 2016* is a fine example.

Barking up the Right Tree 2016

Paul Kavanagh

Vagabond Voices
Glasgow

First published 31 October 2016 by
Vagabond Voices Publishing Ltd.,
Glasgow,
Scotland.

ISBN 978-1-908251-72-5

Printed and bound in Poland

Cover design by Mark Mechan

Typeset by Park Productions

For further information on Vagabond Voices, see the website,
www.vagabondvoices.co.uk

To my mother Martha, who taught me that if you want something done you need to do it yourself.

Barking up the
Right Tree 2016

It's all pain and no gain in the Union now

Thirteen months have passed since the referendum. Thirteen months of faster, safer constitutional change. But despite the promises of the No campaign, Scotland still has not received a single one of the extra super-duper superpowers that were going to be delivered to Holyrood faster than the Flash with an amphetamine habit. Not even the one about road signs. Westminster has stuck us at the STOP sign while it deals with more pressing matters, like the destruction of the NHS, the impoverishment of the low-paid, and getting involved in another war in the Middle East.

But we do have to admit that the claims and promises of the No campaign have indeed come true. It's just that what's come true has been the disasters that they said would befall the NHS, pensions and jobs if we voted Yes. The Tories are taking an axe to the NHS in England, so if you believe that they're going to keep funding the NHS in Scotland when they won't pay for their own then you probably think that the Scottish government has listed Freddy Krueger as a named person. The truth is that with the Tories in government, the Scottish NHS is as safe as a drunk man using a fuse box as a urinal, your pension is as guaranteed as a Rolex watch from the Barras, and your job is as secure as the screw that's loose in the head of anyone who still believes Westminster's promises to treat Scotland with respect. Mind you, Michelle Mone said she'd leave Scotland if there was a Yes vote; there was a No vote and she left anyway. So it's not all bad.

Although none of the goodies have shown up, what we did get delivered was the closure of the Scottish steel industry that the same Better Together campaign told us would only be safe if we voted No. Only the UK had the economic and financial clout needed to protect jobs, they said, even though the UK's economic policy for the past few decades has consisted of clouting the poor to finance the rich. We need the broad shoulders of the UK, they said, though all those broad shoulders ever do is shrug.

This hasn't stopped Kezia and other members of the Holyrood Labour front bench posing for a photo op in Motherwell claiming they were standing with the steelworkers. Let's be kind and say that they weren't actually being duplicitous opportunists, they just got confused between steel and brass necks. Labour posing as the defender of the Scottish steel industry is like one of the trolls who yells "jump" at a depressive on a window ledge posing as a spokesperson for the Samaritans.

No one is seriously claiming that voting No is the direct cause of the closure of the steel plants, but the No campaign claimed that the steel industry needed the strength and security of the UK in order to assure its future. That claim lies discarded in the slag heap along with the credibility of the politicians who made it. It's not just that the UK couldn't protect the working people of Scotland from a toothless gerbil inside a hamster ball, the UK government is leading the assault on their rights and their futures and is far more interested in limiting the powers of Scotland than extending them. They've got no intention of protecting us, and they're doing their damnedest to ensure that we can't protect ourselves. What's next for Scotland? Whatever the Tories decide, and there's nothing we can do about it. It's the Westminster way.

This week another limitation on the rights of Scotland was subject to a report from a committee in the Commons, as Westminster considers whether to make Scottish MPs toothless in law as well as in fact. The Commons will be considering English Votes for English Laws, which is more accurately known as English Votes for Everyone Else's Laws. The Tories want to turn the House of Commons into an English parliament which will also have the final say on UK legislation. Despite the hand-wringing claims about how 533 English MPs get ganged up on and bullied by fifty-nine Scottish ones, the measure is not really about ensuring better democracy for England so much as it's an attempt by the Tories to screw over the Labour Party – although to be fair the Labour Party is doing that perfectly well all by itself and doesn't really need any assistance. But as is always the case, short-term party politicking substitutes for principle in the UK.

The measures will mean that the Speaker of the Commons, previously a strictly apolitical role, will now become highly politicised as he or she will have the power to decide what is or is not a purely "English only" piece of legislation. The government's plans have been described by Shadow Secretary of State for Scotland Ian Murray as an incomprehensible mess. The honourable member for Red Morningside only occupies the post of Shadow Secretary of State for Scotland on the back of English votes for the Labour Party and not Scottish votes, and represents a party which says it's opposed to austerity and Trident but can't bring itself to vote against them. He clearly knows a lot about incomprehensible messes.

The main effect of the new rules will be to relegate Scottish MPs to second-class status. If the Speaker rules that legislation is "English only" then Scottish MPs will not be allowed to vote on it, not even if – like changes to the English NHS – it could potentially have a knock-on effect on the Scottish budget. No Scottish MP will ever be able to hold one of the major offices of state, because they won't be able to vote with the government on important issues that only affect England. Gordie Broon is really upset about it, mainly because it means that no Scottish MP will ever get to be UK prime minister ever again. Although after Gordie's tenure in office that was never going to happen anyway.

It doesn't matter what Scotland's MPs say about EVEL when it's debated in the Commons today. Just like the steel industry, we'll get what the Tories want. That's what Labour and Gordie voted for. If we want Scotland's representatives to decide Scotland's future, we'll have to vote for independence.

22 October 2015

Kezia Dugdale's new tilt for freedom is a futile bid

This week, the Labour Party in Scotland made a brave break for freedom. Despite assuring us all ever since Johann Lamont was elected branch manager that the Labour Party in Scotland had all the independence that the Labour Party doesn't want Scotland to have, it turns out that all this time Labour's idea of letting its Scottish party loose was meant in the same sense as the screw that they believe is loose in Scottish voters' heads. That screw is currently rattling around in the void that passes for the party's sense of purpose.

Johann swore blind that under her, Labour in Scotland was totally autonomous, right up until she resigned claiming she was treated like a branch manager. Johann was fed up that the party HQ in London allowed Labour in Scotland as much freedom as a parent allows a hyperactive toddler to play with a fuse box, and for much the same reasons. Without adult supervision Labour in Scotland can't be trusted with a plastic spoon.

After Johann finally got fed up of Jim Murphy making press statements calling on members of the Labour Party to stop smearing one another while he smeared his way into her job, Jim told everyone that he was the man in charge in Scotland. I make all the decisions, said Jim as he stood on his Irn-Bru crate and dictated policy to party HQ in London in the pages of the papers. The act lasted as long as it took Chuka Umunna to chuck Jim under the wheels of Labour's battlebus during the election campaign. Jim did successfully free Labour in Scotland in one respect however: he freed it from almost all its Westminster seats, and then the party had to try and free itself from Jim, who was clinging on to his non-job with all the determination of a Labour MP in search of an expenses form.

For the past four years Labour in Scotland has been claiming that it's got all the autonomy it could possibly need, but now all of a sudden we discover that Kezia is claiming that Labour in Scotland is autonomouser than ever. Autonomouser than a cat with its own cat flap, but it still drops presents of proposals that are deader than a decapitated rat at our feet as though they were something we really needed and wanted. So is Kezia admitting that all this time Labour in Scotland hasn't really been autonomous at all? The cat's got her tongue.

Kezia has even produced a hand-signed document that Jeremy Corbyn has signed up to too. It's just like Gordie's pre-referendum vow, and just like Gordie's vow Kezia's vow is a vacuous list of vagueness that doesn't promise anything in particular. There's nothing specific in the document that's been paraded in the press, which means that its signatories can claim that it's been fulfilled because it has been designed not to mean anything concrete at all. It's just a last-gasp bit of window dressing to pretend that something significant has happened when everything remains exactly the same as before. So it's exactly like Gordie's vow then.

Kezia's cunning plan is that it's Jeremy Corbyn's leadership of the Labour Party that's going to attract Scottish voters back to the Labour Party, but only if the Labour Party is independent of Jeremy Corbyn. Kezia wants her party to make progress in Scotland by promising things that the party in the rest of the UK isn't going to back, which means that there is zero chance of them ever being put into law. Even if Labour in Scotland was to decide it was opposed to Trident renewal after all, Scotland would still be overruled by MPs from the rest of the UK and we'd get Trident imposed on us anyway.

The real reason Jeremy Corbyn has signed up to the Scottish autonomy plans is because it means that's one less screw-up for him to be blamed for. He's already carrying the can for plenty of those as it is. He really doesn't need to be responsible for James Kelly's charisma bypass or Jackie Baillie's tangential relationship to the truth as well. The Holyrood elections in May next year look like being as much a disaster for the party as last May's Westminster election. There's a very real possibility that Labour will lose all its constituency seats and will be left only with the list seats that the party hierarchy once disdained. The Corbyn bounce in Scotland has had all the success of a spacehopper full of crap. But that's not a nice thing to say about George Foulkes.

If Labour in Scotland really wants to restore its credibility, it needs to divorce itself completely from the UK party and stand on a platform of devo max. That's real devo max, and not the Gordie Broon variety. But there's as much chance of that happening as there is of James Kelly discovering a personality or Kezia Dugdale getting through an interview without managing to say how bad the SNP are. For all Labour's constant renewal and renovation, we're still stuck with the same old faces spouting the same old SNPbad.

After spending the referendum campaign banging on about solidarity, Labour has been divided in its response to the plans, and some of the party's English MPs have reacted to the proposals as though they were being asked to oppose the Tories properly instead of just abstaining. They're afraid that if the Scottish party gets autonomy it might abstain differently and put them in a bad light. Although if Labour in Scotland is capable of putting you in a bad political light then all hope is already lost and you'd be as well heading off to a clinic in Switzerland.

The only way that this plan could represent something radically new would be if Labour in Scotland was able to present different policies from UK Labour during UK elections. But in order to do that electoral law says they'd have to be a different and distinct party. That's not going to happen. Labour in Scotland has always been able to determine its own policies on devolved matters, so what's being proposed now is nothing new, just more window dressing in a shop whose shelves are bare and whose customers have gone elsewhere.

29 October 2015

Dive, dive ... Labour sinks itself on Trident

Labour's Scottish conference has discovered that the party has a soul after all, and voted against the renewal of Trident which also had the effect of making Labour the first quantum party in the UK. Immediately after Labour in Scotland decided it was against Trident, the party's defence spokesperson Maria Eagle reminded them that defence is a reserved matter and Labour is in favour of renewing Trident so shut up, sit down and get back into your radioactive shortbread tin. Scotland's MSPs voted overwhelmingly to oppose Trident renewal. Our MPs are likewise overwhelmingly opposed to Trident renewal. But we'll get Trident renewal anyway.

Maria represents Labour's quantum of soul loss, and Labour is now simultaneously against renewing Trident and in favour of it. It's a bit like Schrödinger's cat, which was famously either alive or dead at the same time, only in Labour's case we know that the cat is definitely dead and definitely not bouncing like Tigger.

Although the party's policy on Trident is far from certain, it's pretty certain that whatever Scotland wants and what her elected representatives vote for will have as much effect on the outcome as a protestor outside the Tory Party conference. Because that's what Scotland's place is in the UK: an entire nation reduced to holding a placard outside a meeting we're not invited to and to which we are not welcome. Maria Eagle thanked Labour in Scotland for their input into the debate, but made it clear that the decision was not going to be made in the country which must play host to the weapons. Trident isn't based on Maria's doorstep, it's based on yours and mine.

Just about the only thing less certain than Labour's actual policy on Trident is how many jobs depend on the UK's nukes. During a Commons debate in February 2005, Geoff Hoon, then Secretary of State for Defence, said that there were 966 Scottish jobs which depended on Trident directly or indirectly. A few years later and following a freedom of information request, the MoD said it was 520 civilian jobs. Jackie Baillie, Labour MSP for Dumbarton, says that 13,000 jobs depend on Trident, although last year she said it was 11,000. Jackie hasn't explained where the extra jobs have come from, but clearly she's a woman who thinks mass destruction is a job creation scheme. It certainly is for politicians, although it won't save Jackie's job during the Scottish elections next year. Jackie ought to be working for Iain Duncan Smith's Department for Work and Pensions who likewise thinks that creating devastation is good for a person's employment prospects. If you think a weapon of mass destruction is a job creation scheme then you probably think that demolishing a house is the best way to redecorate the living room.

Jackie Baillie voted with the Tories in favour of Trident renewal. The vote in Scotland doesn't matter, said Jackie, making a case for independence without realising it. Jackie hasn't understood that no one is proposing to close Faslane down. The SNP wants the base as the HQ of a Scottish navy; Labour wants to diversify the defence industry and repurpose the facilities – a measure the SNP supports as long as Scotland remains in the UK. So all of Jackie's protests were hot air based on a misunderstanding, which is also a good summary of her career to date.

Labour's Trident policy has more kinks than Davie Cameron on a pig farm, and as if that wasn't bad enough, Labour-controlled Glesca Cooncil has apparently decided that its own party is a terrorist threat. Earlier this week it was revealed that the cooncil recently held a Protect Against Terrorism training course for its staff, during which anti-nuclear campaigners were identified as a potential terrorist threat. You'd think that a weapon capable of evaporating the Clyde basin might be the real threat, but the cooncil isn't too bothered about the risk of the city being flattened by a nuclear explosion at Faslane as this would provide opportunities for lots of property developers. Glesca Cooncil thinks the really dangerous risk to the well-being of society is a wee pensioner giving out CND leaflets. Although admittedly there is a risk of paper cuts. On the other hand, there's an even higher risk of Glesca Cooncil being a threat to common sense and human decency.

During the independence referendum campaign the argument was frequently aired that Scotland couldn't get rid of Trident and still be a member of NATO. It's nice to see that Labour has now acknowledged that its former argument isn't true. It's not true and was never true, and moreover can be demonstrated to be untrue, although our Unionist media neglected to point it out at the time.

There's another country which got rid of nukes and submarines and then went on to join NATO. Spain once hosted US Polaris nukes and submarines at the US naval base at Rota near Cadiz, but in the late 1970s as Spain transitioned to democracy following the death of the dictator Franco, Spain negotiated with the USA for the missiles to be removed. The missiles went within two years, and when Spain completed its democratisation process, the country joined NATO – despite the pre-election pledge of the government of Felipe González that Spain would remain neutral. Irrespective of your views on NATO membership, the only surprising thing about the argument that we can't get rid of Trident as it's not compatible with NATO membership is that the argument still gets airtime. If ever you do see the argument in print or on the telly ever again, you can sit back in the knowledge that the only thing it does mean is that those concerned haven't done their research.

Labour's position on Trident is as confused as Jackie Baillie with a teach yourself arithmetic book. So let's make it simple. Essentially the party's position on Trident can be boiled down to the following – we want to be a part of the UK but we don't want UK policy to apply to Scotland because the SNP are bad and it's all their fault. Actually, that's pretty much Labour in Scotland's policy on everything.

5 November 2015

Scotland Bill and the new lows of Labour

It's one thing when Davie Cameron sells you a pig in a poke, after all he's the prime minister who infamously poked a pig, allegedly. But it's something else entirely when the pig you're being sold turns out to be inedible rancid bacon that is unfit for porcine purpose. That's the Scotland Bill, which drooled its way through Westminster this week like a year-old slice of ham oozing its way down to the bottom of a bin where it could rest with the Tory and Labour recovery that's always about to happen.

The Scotland Bill is hailed by Westminions as Westminster's response to the independence referendum. That's the referendum that they feel the need to keep reminding everyone that they won because they can feel their victory slipping out of their grasp. The bill was never intended as a definitive and final response to the demands of the people of Scotland for increased powers for the Scottish parliament, it was meant as the minimum that could appease enough of the people of Scotland to ensure that independence remains the preferred option of a minority of Scots. At least for the time being. The time being being defined as Davie Cameron's period in office because then he won't go into the history books as the prime minister who broke the Union as well as being the one who was forced to deny overfamiliarity with a dead pig.

However whether or not Davie has buggered off out of office when the Union falls apart, he won't escape responsibility for being the prime minister who was in charge when the Unionist parties undercut the foundations of the very Union they claim to support. Fixated on the referendum result, they overlooked the two-part message from the Scottish electorate. The referendum was the Union being given a last chance, the general election was a reminder that Scotland expects her demands to be met. But all you could hear from the Westminster chamber this week was the hear hear bray of a Tory posho who's not listening and the Labour donkeys doing his dirty work.

Every time you think that Labour can't stoop any lower, that they've already broken through the bottom of the barrel in the basement and are now somewhere down in the bedrock with the dinosaurs, the party breaks the laws of physics again. They go lower than a limbo dancer who's had an argument with a road roller, they break the Joyce Barrier – going so low that Eric Joyce could lecture them from the moral high ground. After spending the past fortnight demanding that the Scottish government do something to protect the low-paid in Scotland from the Tory cut to tax credits, the Labour Party went and voted with the Tories to prevent the devolution of tax credits to the Scottish parliament.

It was an astonishing act of political self-harm, more hypocritical than Tony Blair at the Remembrance Sunday ceremony making like he mourned the deaths he's responsible for. The Tories were going to vote down allowing Scotland any real power to protect itself from Tory cuts. Labour could have done its usual abstention act, and washed its hands and wept false tears and tried to pretend that abstention was better than a cure. Labour's only a latent opposition party, only latent isn't better than never.

If Labour had abstained Kezia could have gone on the telly and claimed that Labour was trying to defend the low-paid and blamed it on the Tories, but you know, more importantly, SNPbad. Now she needs to explain to the people of Scotland why Labour thinks it's more important that the Scottish government should find the funding for a bandage for the low-paid, but her party voted alongside the Tories to allow Westminster to chop their legs off, and why it is that Labour voted for the legs to be cut off. Thankfully for Kezia, our largely Unionist media doesn't believe in asking her difficult questions, by which is meant any question which can't be answered by saying SNPbad. Although that's never stopped her before. Only in the Unionist media is there nothing but the sound of silence when it comes to the Scotland Bill, a sure sign that they know it's rubbish and that if the proceedings in Westminster this week were advertised to the people of Scotland we'd be demanding independence by Friday.

The choice facing Labour was between devolving tax credits and avoiding the Tory cuts entirely, or not devolving them and then trying to mitigate the cuts by complicated and expensive means which might not even have the desired effect. The

Fundillymundell pointedly refused to answer a direct question on whether his government would classify tax credit top-ups from the Scottish as income, and claw them back by reducing other benefits or by treating it as taxable. That's pretty much a guarantee that that's precisely what they intend to do. So the Scottish block grant gets cut, the low-paid have their tax credits cut, the Scottish government tries to make up the difference by cutting other services or raising tax, then Westminster claws the top-up back sucking even more cash from Scotland that it can use to give tax breaks to the companies that won't pay their workers living wages in the first place.

The tax credits debacle is the Scotland Bill in miniature. Scotland gets nothing useful from the process, just tax powers that are deliberately framed so they affect punters on low and middle incomes. Taxes on the rich and on big companies remain the preserve of Westminster. Scotland can raise taxes on low and medium earners in order to soften the worst of the Tory cuts, but can't raise taxes on the rich and the big companies who benefit most from those Tory cuts.

And that's just fine with a Labour Party that is so terrified of devolution that it can't even bring itself to devolve powers over abortion to a parliament where the three main parties are led by women. Labour prefers the power to remain with a parliament whose representatives have such a deep understanding of women's reproductive rights that they think tampons are a luxury.

It was reported this week that the Queen said there are "more Scots" in Westminster after fifty-six SNP

MPs were returned to Parliament. Labour's Scots were quiet and meek and did their best not to be noticed. That's Scotland's place in the Union, quiet and timid and don't raise your voice. They're a party of cereal eaters. But Labour's timidity and fear of the power of the Scottish people killed it this week, and together with the Tories they killed the Union too.

12 November 2015

The truth of why we lost the referendum won't kill our dream of independence

So the case for independence is dead, again. Former SNP policy chief Alex Bell has published some criticisms of the SNP's economic policy for independence, and all of a sudden there's no case for independence any more. The case for independence has died more often than the Dalai Lama or the leader of the Labour Party in Scotland, both of whom are then promptly reincarnated – although the Labour leader also gets to die in Holyrood every week at First Minister's Questions. Either the case for independence will be born again, or like the famously premature obituary of Mark Twain, reports of its death are exaggerated. I'm going to go with the latter.

The media debate during the fevered few months leading up to September last year focused almost exclusively on the economic case for independence, so essentially the argument for independence was won or lost on pounds and pence. That's all the Unionist media wanted to talk about, that's all Scotland was allowed to talk about. There was almost no attention paid to the moral case for Scotland removing nuclear weapons from its soil, only to the financial cost in an arguable number of jobs which were inflated larger than Jackie Baillie's ego. There was no attention paid to the social benefits of land reform, all we heard was that big companies would flee in terrror from a country whose citizens dared to assert their own destiny. We were told that a nation exists to service the economy, and not that an economy exists to service a nation.

It's obvious to everyone that the economic case for independence which was put forward by the SNP during the independence campaign was flawed. Those flaws were flayed open by a biased and partial media all throughout the campaign. We all know that there were problems in the arguments because the arguments failed to persuade a majority of Scotland's voters. In that respect, what Alex Bell said was not surprising, and was nothing new. He's been making similar points for quite a while.

What Alex Bell most definitely didn't say was what certain sections of the Scottish media are reporting he said. He didn't say that there is no longer a case for independence. He criticised parts of the SNP's prospectus. Despite the fond wishes of the Unionist commentariat, what the SNP says is not the same as the case for independence. Other models are available. Alex Bell wants us to look at these other models; the Unionist parties would prefer to turn his remarks into a death spin for independence.

What Alex Bell did say was that there are economic obstacles to a prosperous independent Scotland, and he added that these were problems which could be overcome. That's not quite the same thing as saying that there is no longer a case for independence and we should knuckle down under the permausterity of Osborne and accept the job cuts and the axe that's being taken to public services and the common good so that big companies can make bigger profits and pay their executives even bigger bonuses. But hey, at least we'll still be able to watch *Great British Bake Off* and feel our hearts swell with pride as all those workers whose jobs were supposed to be safe if Scotland voted No are made redundant and cast before the not so tender mercies of Jobcentre sanctions.

Then there are the arguments for independence which can't easily be reduced to a financial balance sheet, spread out and pinned down in Excel like a dead butterfly in a cabinet. Yet those arguments never got a look-in. Arguments about democracy, about holding our political classes to account, about a written constitution, about self-respect, about Scotland deciding for itself what is good for Scotland – the Unionist media didn't want to discuss those arguments, and still doesn't want to discuss them today. They're too busy crowing that the case for independence is dead because someone who was once an advisor in the SNP has stated the obvious in public – that the economic case for independence was less than perfect. Well colour me surprised.

The Unionist media and political parties have leapt on Alex Bell's measured and careful criticisms of parts of the independence case like a pack of hyenas at an end of season sale at a butcher's. It's not even like Alex Bell's criticisms are new: he made similar points in 2013, and they were likewise hailed by sections of the Unionist media as signalling the death of the case for independence. But the only thing that has died for good here is the credibility of Unionist commentary.

Even the smallest of criticisms from within the Yes campaign are seized upon and magnified into a death blow for independence. And then the selfsame Unionist media and parties bewail the polarisation of Scottish politics, while all the time they create the very conditions that cause Yes supporters to close ranks and not give an inch – because if we do then all of a sudden there are banner headlines declaring that the case for independence has died again. But the death of independence has been heralded as often as the rebirth of Labour in Scotland. Neither is going to happen any time soon. The cause of independence remains as vibrant as Labour is moribund, and no amount of Unionist spinning is going to change that fact.

All the Unionist parties offer is stagnation and mitigation, no road out of the mess we're in and no means to protect ourselves from the viciousness of uncaring Tory governments that we didn't vote for. What happened in September last year was that Scotland was asked to consider the price of independence, but not to consider its value. The value of independence remains like a bright shining beacon in the darkness of a long Tory night where hope is extinguished with every benefits sanction, with every job that's lost. The SNP's prospectus may be flawed, as Alex Bell claims, but that still won't dent support for the party no matter how much the newspapers publish the obituary of independence. Independence offers a way out, and a poor road is always going to be better than no road at all. If the choice is between taking your chances with Nicola, or remaining in the mire with Kezia, it's a no-brainer.

19 November 2015

Bomb first, think later is no plan for peace

So here we go again, amidst dire warnings of terror-
ists who are about to get their evil paws on nukes and
missiles, Britain looks set to engage in military action
in Syria. We've been here before, but this time it's
the so-called Islamic State, which is to Islam as the
witchfinders and torturing inquisitors of the sixteenth
century were to Christianity – people who believe
in all the fundamentals of their faith except the bits
that call for kindness, compassion and empathy.

Last time it was Gaddafi, the time before it was
Saddam Hussein. There's always another evil stalk-
ing the face of the planet which is always the greatest evil imaginable, until another unimaginable
set of horrors stalks along. The UK always has to
get involved in the name of bringing about a lasting peace that is as elusive as Iain Duncan Smith's
sense of compassion. Whatever the crisis, whatever
the tragedy, the UK's knee-jerk response is military
intervention. Refugee crisis? Bomb something. Bomb
first, think later, plan for the future not at all.

Peace never comes to the UK, and it never will. In
the 308 years since the Kingdom of Scotland joined
with the Kingdom of England to create the United
Kingdom, there have been around just sixty years
during which Britain has not been involved in some

war, in "police action", or in suppressing an insurgency campaign. War is the norm for the UK, periods of peace are the aberration. During the eighteenth and nineteenth centuries there were the countless wars of colonialism, which included acts of genocide like the destruction of the native Tasmanians, but things didn't get much better in the troubled twentieth century. The peace dividend in the twenty-first has been even worse, with military action in Sierra Leone, Iraq, Afghanistan, Libya, and now most likely Syria.

There was only one war when the British were the unalloyed and undisputed good guys, and that was when the opponents were the actual Nazis. Most of the rest of the time British service people were dying in the cause of propping up dubious regimes, or deposing dictators and leaving chaos and destruction in their wake. Saddam Hussein was an evil murderer, but even more people have died in the war to depose him and the anarchy that has followed. You don't save lives by killing more people.

The tragedy is that none of this is new, none of this is unexpected. For eighty per cent of the entire length of time that the United Kingdom has been in existence, British armed forces have been killing or being killed somewhere around the globe. If the purpose of the British armed services is to bring peace and stability, the Ministry of Defence and our political masters are making spectacularly ill-use of them. The armed forces get sent off to do Westminster's bidding, then the wounded and maimed and the mentally ill come home to rely on charity and an increasingly threadbare social security net that's more hole than net.

According to the Stop the War campaigning group, twenty-six per cent of former service people suffer from mental health issues, ten per cent of prisoners previously served in the armed forces, and an estimated nine thousand homeless people are former soldiers – one in ten of rough sleepers. Whitehall is serving us badly, and serving the servicemen and women even worse. The British state waves a few poppies in November and then sends more off to fight and die.

Yet Britain's official discussion of defence revolves around how big and powerful the toys given to the MoD are going to be. This week the SNP called for a vote in the Commons on the renewal of the ruinously expensive civilisation ruining machines of Trident. Trident serves no purpose other than to prop up the UK's claim to big power status. Claiming that nuclear missiles have kept the peace for the past fifty years is patently untrue in a country which has been involved in wars for most of those years. But even if the UK had not been involved in any conflicts at all, it still wouldn't mean that nukes were responsible. That's like claiming that having a ginger dug in your house is an effective Nessie deterrent. Since getting the dug I have not once seen a loch monster in my living room, so obviously the dug deterrent is working. Correlation is not causation, as any good nuclear scientist will tell you. Clearly the politicians haven't been listening.

During the debate, Labour opposed the Tories by abstaining. It's now the default position of the Labour Party to abstain, a position that owes more to the deep cracks within the party. Labour's representatives are more interested in opposing one another than they are in doing the job they were elected to do, which is to oppose the Tories. But it wasn't all labstaining: fourteen Labour MPs did a Jackie Baillie and voted with the Conservative government, while six rescued a moral conscience and voted with the SNP against Trident renewal. The rest of the party, including the entire shadow cabinet, bravely ran away while claiming that the SNP only wanted the debate in the first place so that they could say nasty things about the Labour Party.

Lifelong CND supporter Jeremy Corbyn also abstained on the question of renewing Trident missiles. Since becoming party leader he's been infected with the SNPbad virus and develops a case of Kezitis whenever it looks like he's got to vote in the same lobby as the SNP. So it's now clear that Labour's hierarchy of opposition runs as follows – first they oppose each other, then they oppose the SNP, and third and finally they'll oppose the Tories but only if it doesn't conflict with opposing the other two.

Labour offers as much protection against the Tories as covering Glesca City Chambers with a layer of marshmallows would protect the city against the radioactive fallout from an accident at Faslane. That's why they're going to get chewed up at next year's Holyrood elections. Scotland desperately needs a decent and effective Opposition, Labour isn't it.

26 November 2015

Does it suit the Tories for Gaelic to die out?

Hidden away in George Osborne's autumn statement the other week was a wee item which, if we had a properly functioning media in Scotland, ought to have attracted far more criticism than it did. Although Georgie managed to find extra money for weapons of mass destruction and for a bombing campaign in Syria which will put civilian lives at risk in return for purely cosmetic political effects, he decided that the UK government will no longer fund Gaelic broadcasting in Scotland.

You might think that the future of the Gaelic language is not important, that it's of low priority and we shouldn't be discussing it when far weightier matters are at stake. But there is always going to be something that someone, generally an English language monoglot, will consider of greater importance than Scotland's ancient language, a language that the critics already decry as dead. The fact is that if we do not take serious and sustained action now to save the Gaelic language, then it will die. There is no free market in language. Languages live or die according to the support given to them by the powerful and the influential. It's obvious that the Tory government isn't going to give the Gaelic language and an important part of Scottish culture the support it needs to survive. The only conclusion is that they don't care if it lives or dies, and even that it might suit them for it to die out, then they can argue that Scotland doesn't have a language or culture of its own.

So much for the respect agenda then. Scotland's ancient culture isn't respected enough for Osborne to find even the token amount of funding previously granted to it by a UK government which jealously hoards control of broadcasting like Smaug. But some things are clearly more precious than keeping Scottish culture alive, things like tax breaks for rich corporations and bombing raids on Syria.

You'd think that the Tories would show Gaelic a bit more consideration. After all, at least according to the enraged response from certain Unionists on Twitter recently, the Gaelic language is so powerful that simply painting two Gaelic words on the side of a police helicopter stops it from working. Meanwhile bilingual Gaelic signage in train stations has the power to confuse and alienate poor wee English monoglots. To some folk, Gaelic is a dead language and with their mockery and disdain they're going to do their utmost to ensure that it dies. Some people need to look up the meaning of the phrase self-fulfilling prophecy.

In the modern world a language needs broadcast media to survive. Broadcasting is a reserved matter. The Unionist parties are united in their refusal to consider devolving control of television or radio to Holyrood, even broadcasting in Gaelic or Scots. Obviously whether *Postman Pat* is dubbed into Gaelic is a matter of such fundamental importance that it requires the input of a Tory MP from Bedfordshire. Of course the real reason that Westminster won't devolve control of Gaelic broadcasting, or the Scots broadcasting that it doesn't allow at all, is that such devolution would leads to demands for the devolution of English language broadcasting too. That would threaten the Unionist hegemony, and Scotland might insist that since Scotland raises £335 million in TV licence fees then we expect rather more than the £35 million currently spent on Scottish TV production. Under the Union your TV licence fee has to go on *Great British Sycophancy* with Nicholas Witchell instead.

Westminster insists it retains control of Gaelic language broadcasting, but it's not going to pay for it. Gaelic is a rich and evocative language, a cursory trawl through a Gaelic dictionary produces at least six words for hypocrisy – *beul-chràbhadh, breug-chràbhadh, cealg, cealgaireachd, fìmeanachd, saobh* – but that still isn't enough to describe the duplicitous double-dealing of the UK government where Scotland and her culture are concerned. If Westminster wants to call the tune, then it needs to pay the piper.

Westminster previously granted a mere £1 million annually to BBC Alba for Gaelic broadcasting in Scotland. The rest of the channel's funding comes from the BBC, which pays £8 million, and from the Scottish government – which despite having no legal responsibility for broadcasting coughs up almost £14 million a year for a public service which remains controlled and regulated by Westminster. £1 million isn't much in terms of UK government spending.

According to a recent report on Sky News, £1 million will also be the average cost of a single RAF bombing raid on Syria. It's clear where the priorities of the UK government lie. George Osborne would far rather dish out death and destruction than deliver *Dotaman*. There's always plenty money for bombs, never enough for culture and education.

Gaelic television only exists because of a treaty commitment by the UK government. Westminster signed up to the European Charter for Regional or Minority Languages which has a number of different chapters specifying varying degrees of protection for threatened languages like Gaelic and Scots. Westminster decided to give Gaelic greater protection than Scots, and part of that meant that at European level the UK government committed itself to providing Gaelic language broadcasting. Now having made the commitment, Westminster is refusing to pay for it.

Westminster didn't make the same commitment with respect to Scots. There's no linguistic or cultural reason for the difference in treatment; the difference is political. A significant number of Scottish politicians, and a public which the same politicians have ensured have never been educated about Scottish languages, doesn't accept that Scots is a "proper language". Yet there is no controversy amongst linguists. Linguists accept the status of Scots as a language.

Scottish politicians and journalists who refuse to accept that Scots is a real language are the linguistic equivalent of creationist fundamentalists who maintain that there is a scientific controversy about the theory of evolution. There's no controversy amongst biologists or palaeontologists, there's only controversy amongst people who have a political reason for refusing to educate themselves.

The same holds true for Scottish languages, but the flat earthers and creationists of language science are the people who determine Scottish broadcasting and education policy. The Union is a death sentence for Scottish languages, and a death sentence for Scottish culture, killed by the smug Smaug Tories who'd rather pay for war.

3 December 2015

Could Donald Trump, the Hairball of Hypocrisy, really be US prez?

It's been a good week for wind farms, and a bad week. The bad news is that the Tories are doing their utmost to screw over the renewable energy industry which could secure Scotland's future prosperity. Better together eh. Seems it meant better together as a dependant. Better together means never being able to look after yourself. It's a bit like being told that you're better off with Dracula, because then at least you know you'll have a regular diet of flies as your lifeblood is sucked away and you descend into the madness regularly displayed in the columns of the *Daily Mail*.

It wasn't all bad news, Katie Hopkins's new chat show has been axed, proving that there is a god after all, but the good news for wind farms wasn't so much good for renewable energy as it was good news for *Schadenfreude*. The Great Fake Tan of Global Trolling, the Hairball of Hypocrisy, Donald Trump got trumped by the UK Supreme Court, who told him that the fact that the turbines might muss up his hair was not legal grounds for an objection. Anyway, the man who has inflicted tasteless monstrosities like Trump Towers on the world has no right to complain about a view being ruined. It costs a huge amount of money to look as cheap as a Donald Trump development. Besides, Donald is the only person on the planet who doesn't have to look at Donald, so if anything it's the rest of humanity which has a legal case about objectionable monstrosities hoving into sight. Donald, being unable to accept no as an answer, has said he'll take the case to Europe, but it's unlikely to succeed as his claim is as overblown as his hair and his claims about his achievements. If he'd just stuck his father's fortune in the bank and lived off the interest, he'd be richer now than he actually is. All Donald's business acumen has done has been to lose money. He's a spoiled rich kid failure who overcompensates with an inflated ego.

Donald thinks that now that Barack Obama has established that it's possible for a person of colour to become president, then the way is cleared for him. People with bright orange fake tans are America's oppressed minority. There are carrots which look pale and wan in comparison. He thought the slogan of the civil rights movement was "We shall overcomb."

Trump's greatest political achievement is to make Jeb Bush seem like a sensible moderate – that and proving why we really are right to be afraid of clowns. Donald's bid to become prez of the US hasn't suffered because of his outrageous promise to ban all Muslims from travel to the States. It's only foreigners of a liberal tendency who are outraged, and since we're the kind of people he wants to ban, that's not hurting his chances any. The petition to ban him from the UK has received a lot of support in North

East Scotland, as they're ones who suffer the most from his trips here.

While it would be great if we could make sure that we never had to see him again, Trump's mother was born in Scotland which means that he has a right to dual US-UK citizenship. It might not be legally possible to ban him from entry to the UK. He'd likely retaliate by banning entry to the US not just to Muslims, but to all Scottish people, people who work for wind turbine manufacturers, anyone who possesses a full head of hair, and anyone who has ever been in the same room as Alex Salmond.

Despite the fact that he says he wants to control immigration but can't even control his own hair, Trump's popularity has shot up amongst Americans who love their constitutional right to shoot things up, white middle-class men who feel victimised, and people who think that Fox News really is balanced and fair. Thankfully such people don't make up a majority of Americans, but the US presidential election is now centred around the existential question, toupee or not toupee.

The big problem is that the other contenders for the Republican candidacy are so utterly utterly woeful. They're plastic politicians of the religious right machine variety, people whose solution to the epidemic of mass shootings in the USA is to offer to pray for the victims, outright homophobes, creationists, and fantasists whose grasp on reality is even more tenuous than Donald Trump's. Yes, the scary thing is that in the USA that is actually possible. Against that lot, billionaire Donald, pal of the corporations, can pose as the outsider.

It's looking as though America may be facing a choice next year between Donald Trump for the Republicans and Hillary Clinton for the Democrats. Clinton is as loathed by the Republicans as Trump is by the rest of the planet, and the election will be the most divisive that America has ever experienced. If you think that the Scottish referendum was characterised by bullying, insults and bad behaviour, you're about to get a lesson in a real political hatefest and a joke that's no longer funny.

19 December 2015

The teacake toothache plot
to steal your mind

The Middle East is in flames again, Europe's no border policy is in tatters, the UK government continues to wreck what passes for a British constitution, the poor and vulnerable are castigated and punished by a Tory government that doesn't care about social justice, and in Scotland's social media people are getting het up about a storm in a teacake.

In case you've been in a confectionary-free cave for the past week, although this being the fag end of the holiday season that's unlikely, the Tunnock's company has announced that it's going to rebrand its archetypal product. Teacakes are a Scottish icon: they danced at the opening of the Commonwealth Games and they inspired the set design for BBC Scotland's flagship current affairs programme that no one watches. But although they are as Scottish as type 2 diabetes and bad teeth, no more will the teacakes sold in the rest of the UK bear the image of a wee Scottish lion. Now they're going to be marketed outwith Scotland as the Great British teacake, because bad teeth and type 2 diabetes are Great British values too.

The news was received with a few complaints on social media, where people like to get upset about small things as it saves the angst of getting upset about the really distressing stuff like the impending war in the Middle East or the fact that many people in Scotland can no longer afford teacakes. A handful of random independence-supporting punters said that they weren't going to buy Tunnock's teacakes any more because if its confectionary doesn't appear to the rest of the world with a statement of Scottishness then they're not going to purchase it. These were the same random independence-supporting punters who had said the exact same thing in 2014 when the company pinned its coloured foil teacake wrappers to the Better Together campaign mast, so the net loss to the company's coffers is going to be precisely zero.

Tunnock's tinfoil wrappers have many uses. The Scottish Unionist media has clearly fashioned them into a lovely hat as it repeatedly claims that the populace have been seduced into a nationalist cult by the evil mind controllers of the SNP. The Unionist media is still in full possession of its teacake-wrapper-based millinery, because as soon as the aforementioned random punters had said they weren't going to buy teacakes, Unionist journalists took to Twitter to denounce the SNP led boycott of a Scottish institution. This was an attempt to create the fear that in an independent Scotland, only state approved confectionary will be permitted. It could even lead to Unionists being deprived of the tinfoil supplies they so desperately need in order to protect themselves from the SNP mind control waves that will be picked up on all the fillings their teeth will require after patriotically stuffing their faces with Great British teacakes. And then the SNP's master plan to create a nation of remote-controlled zombie cultists with unhealthy dentition will be complete.

I don't have any problems with the marketing decisions of a company which is owned by a Conservative supporter who is openly Unionist. It's his company and it's not like his views are a secret. Tunnock's has made a commercial decision which it believes will boost sales, and that's going to benefit jobs in Scotland. This is a good thing. But it's sad that the company thinks it can only boost sales in the rest of the UK by disguising its Scottishness, like Guinness would do better if they pretended not to be Irish. It's sad that it thinks Scottishness isn't a selling point in the rest of the UK whereas in the rest of the world Scotland has a far more positive image than the UK does. Ask people outside the UK what they think of Britain and you'll get a lot of negativity as well as positivity – like the British propensity for invading places, colonialisation and hypocrisy. But ask what they think of Scotland and the only negative is the weather, which is fair enough. I know this because I once conducted a rigorous survey in a pub in Barcelona.

More seriously, the fact that a Scottish company believes that advertising its Scottishness is damaging to its sales in the rest of the UK says something about the place of Scotland in the rest of this Union. It says that Scotland is only acceptable in the UK when it's invisible. And there was me thinking that back in 2014 the Unionists were arguing that you could vote no and still be a proud Scot. In fact they were very determined to tell us all just how proud they were to be Scottish. Proudly proud of their proudScottisness, so they were. Now we discover that they're not quite so proud after all, because if a Unionist-supporting company says if you put a Scottish lion on a tea-cake box it means you're promoting Scottishness not Britishness, then that implies that Scottishness is inimical to Britishness, which is a direct contradiction of what the proud Unionist Scots were saying during the independence campaign. It would seem that you can't be British by virtue of being Scottish after all.

Scotland's proper place in the Union is a silent one. We can be British, but we can only be British by denying that there is anything distinctive about being Scottish, and it's wrong for anyone to get upset by the erasure of Scottish culture. From tea-cakes with rampant lions, through the supposed Britishness of Tudor monarchs who never reigned in Scotland, to complaints about Gaelic language signage, Scotland cannot be allowed to be culturally distinctive in any shape or form. Acknowledging that Scottish culture is real and vital might threaten the racist stereotype that the only reason anyone in Scotland supports independence is because we hate the English. Acknowledging that Scottish culture exists is an acknowledgement that Scotland is a nation, and nations have the right to self-determination.

But none of this is a story. The story in the media is of course that a handful of random punters made noises about no longer buying teacakes. Scotland isn't allowed to define itself, and the Scottish independence movement isn't allowed to define itself either. We need to be defined by the Unionist media. Now sit down, shut up, and eat your Great British teacakes.

6 January 2016

Federalism is just a tired buzzword that won't stop independence

The great and good of the Union, or rather a cross-party grouping of unelected Lords including erst-while firebrand revolutionary turned ermine-wearing expenses claimer Peter Hain, have admitted something that supporters of Scottish independence have known for some time. The Union isn't working.

The Union is going as smoothly as a meeting of the parliamentary Labour Party. It's as believable as a Lib Dem in Orkney. It has all the appeal of a Tory candidate in Calton going door to door offering signed photies of Margaret Thatcher. Although to be fair, you could at least punt the photies on eBay, whereas it's unlikely that you'd get your money back on Peter Hain. Mind you, when a bunch of political placepersons, party donors, appointees and careerists count as the great and good, then you've already pretty much admitted that yer Union is knackered. And the people who're going to make it democratic are the Union's unelected appointees with their expensive expense claims.

The group of Lords have come up with a new set of proposals for a federal settlement which they say will save the UK. More precisely they say it will save the UK from Scottish separatism, even though calling independence separatism is like calling a month-long holiday in the Maldives a day trip to Glasgow Airport. It's like saying you shouldn't go on holiday because there may be a queue at check-in. Independence is a state of being, a state of mind, and a large segment of the Scottish population has already made its own personal declaration of independence from Westminster. That's what's really scaring the Lords: we've got our boarding passes and we're just waiting for the gate to open. They're determined to persuade us that we really want to spend a wet July in Clacton instead.

What these new proposals are really all about is to stave off the inevitability of Scottish independence. There would be no cross-party grouping coming up with bold new ideas to rewrite the British constitution if it were not for the fact that the voters of Scotland are increasingly finding the Unionist parties as attractive an option as dancing naked through a patch of thistles to the accompaniment of "Land of Hope and Glory" while whipping themselves with jaggy nettles, even though it may well be the case that certain members of the Conservative Party enjoy that sort of thing as it's the nearest they get to expressing their Scottishness. But then there are nightclubs for all sorts of tastes.

It's not a coincidence that as Scotland enters an election year sections of the Unionist parties start making noises about federalism. The Westminster parliament refuses to be bound by official party policy or manifesto commitments, so if you think that they're going to follow through on noises made by superannuated politicians who no longer hold any positions of influence, I've got a Vow to sell you. Because that worked out so well for Scotland last time, didn't it.

At least this time the Unionist parties have the decency to make some specific noises as opposed to the vague waffle of the Vow, but the chances that any of this is going to pass into law are about the same as the chances that Alistair Carmichael can get through an election campaign without a smear. There is no point in detailing any of the proposals for super-duper federalism because they're not going to happen, but then making them happen isn't the point of the exercise.

The point of the exercise is to make it look as though something is happening when in fact nothing is happening at all, when what we're really getting is the reverse of federalism, the increasing control of the centre. Lord Salisbury, the former Tory leader of the Lords, said that he hoped the proposals would allow the idea of a federal settlement to be "injected into the political bloodstream" in the run up to the May elections. And there's the truth of it, it's all just a publicity stunt that is meant to distract public attention from the Tories' bid to make their control permanent and to freeze Scotland's MPs out of any decision-making at all.

Just as the Tories are busily cutting constitutional connections to Scotland, along comes a group of Lords suggesting a new foundation to the Union. It gives the supine Unionist media something to talk about, and if all goes well a handful of voters in

Scotland might decide that they haven't quite finished with the Labour Party after all and will give them one more chance to prove themselves.

Meanwhile, as politicians without power or influence, or even votes, mouth platitudes about federalism, the Tory government gets on with the serious business of cutting Scotland out of power. This week we saw the first use of the EVEL rules, which reduced Scotland's MPs to the status of international observers at Westminster. Our MPs are now second-class legislators in a parliament where power is exercised without any possibility that the wishes of the Scottish electorate are taken into account.

The unelected and unaccountable Lords and Ladies on the cross-party grouping can waffle on about a federal UK, but their proposals will go the same way as Gordie Broon's claim that a No vote would give us the closest thing possible to federalism. Proposals for a federal settlement pop up every time the British establishment fears for its future. They jostle for public attention like a Labour Party MSP seeking a place on the list and are every bit as useless.

Every time the Union is thought to be under threat, which is pretty much daily these days, someone at Westminster uses the federalism buzzword, the Westminster abracadabra to magic the nasty nationalists away. Proposals for federalism are the donkey that does the heavy lifting for the Save the Union Brigade, and like a donkey it means hee-haw. The braying of the federalist donkey won't delay the inevitable.

16 January 2016

Twisted tales from Unionist media are laughable

January has been a slow news month. So slow that there's even a dearth of SNPbad stories. It must be pretty desperate when Scotland's Unionist media runs short of things to accuse the SNP of, not that that stops them. They've got so desperate that if you were to go deep down into the lowest sub-basement in a barrel factory and climbed into the barrel at the bottom of the pile of broken rejects, if you listened very carefully you'd hear the sound of a yooney journalist scraping away in the lower levels of Hell underneath.

This week the swivel-eyed cultists of professional yoonery reached a new low, which was quite an achievement considering how low they've gone before. On Thursday the entire front page of one Unionist daily was occupied with the shocking and disgusting news that an SNP MP had spent the Christmas and New Year holidays saving lives and caring for the sick. How very dare she? Imagine having the sheer nerve to treat cancer patients and operate on them when she ought to be sitting on her bum while Parliament is closed just in case the Unionist press decides to attack her for something.

Philippa Whitford is the SNP MP for Central Ayrshire. Before entering politics she worked as a surgeon in the NHS specialising in treating women with breast cancer. For five days over the recent holiday season she covered for a former colleague who was ill, and this was used as the basis of a front-page headline accusing her of profiting from the NHS on top of her MP's salary. It's not exactly as if there is a limitless pool of breast cancer specialists for the NHS to call on, but Philippa was strongly criticised by Jackie Baillie MSP, of all people, for daring to ensure that NHS patients get the treatment they need in a timely fashion.

That would be the same Jackie Baillie who has made a career out of attacking the Scottish government's record on the NHS. It seems that some MSPs are more interested in attacking the SNP than they are in ensuring that NHS patients get the treatment and care that they deserve. Labour gleefully jumps on a Tory media bandwagon, and then they wonder why the wheels have fallen off their support in Scotland.

There are other ways in which the story could have been covered. It could have been written up as, "MP gives up her holidays to ensure that NHS targets are met." Or it might have been reported that a Scottish MP actually did something useful and productive to contribute to the sum total of human good. They're not able to do much of that in Westminster what with being outvoted by the Tories on Scottish legislation and banned from voting on issues that the Tories deem to be English-only. The Unionist media would far rather that our MPs did absolutely nothing.

That would be the same media that never uttered a peep while Tory and Labour MPs enriched themselves with all sorts of second jobs and consultancies. That would be the same media that wasn't overly concerned about the non-attendance in Parliament of former prime minister and saviour of the Union Gordie Broon. But if an SNP MP engages in a socially useful job for just five days over a holiday period when the Westminster parliament is in recess, a job that very few are able to do, then you get a denunciation that even the Spanish Inquisition would feel was a bit excessive. But with the yoon media denunciation cult, you always expect the Inquisition.

Coming just a short while after a full-page splash accusing Nicola Sturgeon of having good taste in raincoats and wellington boots, this latest story damages the media far more than it damages the SNP. All that it proves is that the real blinkered and self-regarding cult in Scottish politics is the narrow wee world of the tragic yoondom which is incapable of seeing anything good in the independence movement. When even giving up your holiday to spend it treating cancer patients to cover for a sick former colleague becomes a reason for criticism, you know that all sense of perspective has been lost. If Philippa had given up her holiday to treat refugees while she stayed in a Buddhist monastery in Cambodia, it would have been reported as "SNP MP jets off to tropical paradise to join foreign cult."

The role of the press is supposedly to inform, to elucidate, to persuade, and to hold the powerful to account. That's not the main task of the Unionist media in Scotland however. Their task is to stave off independence for as long as possible, by any means possible. What they're doing with these ridiculous stories is to give committed Unionists something else to feel aggrieved about.

They constantly claim that the independence movement has divided Scotland, that it looks for grievances to exploit. The Unionist media seeks to deepen those divides and reinforce them. It even manages to turn treating cancer patients into a stick with which to beat the SNP. The real irrational cultists in Scotland are the grievance manufacturers of the Unionist press. The only thing anyone is persuaded of is how unfit for purpose our media has become.

30 January 2016

Scotland must not consent to being ripped off

Time is running out for the Scottish and UK governments to reach an agreement on a financial settlement to underpin the Scotland Act. The actions of Westminster throughout the process have been as duplicitous as their colonialists who went to foreign lands seeking gold and slaves, saying that they'd come in peace. In the family tree of Britain, Westminster expects Scotland to be the sap. Now they're getting upset because Scotland isn't cooperating in the kicking they want to give us.

The Scottish government wants a funding formula that fulfils the conditions of the Smith Commission, that there should be no detriment to Scotland or the rest of the UK in the new financial arrangements to underpin the devolution settlement. This was what the UK government signed up to, and it was one of the core provisions of the watered-down Smith Commission that was itself a watered-down version of the Vow. There's more watering down in the proposals of the UK goverment than drunk men relieving themselves up closes after a Saturday night out in Glasgow, and the Westminster torrent of micturation continues unabated.

The respected economist Prof Anton Muscatelli of the University of Glasgow, who happens to be a Unionist, says that the system preferred by the Scottish government is the one most likely to be safest for both Scotland and the UK. The UK government disagrees. They want a financial settlement that allows Whitehall to screw Scotland over in order to appease the legions of Tory MPs who are convinced that Scotland is funded by English taxpayers. The Tories want a settlement that could result in Scotland losing £3.5 billion in funding on top of the cuts that they're already imposing. That's the Union benefit we were promised by the Better Together campaign during the independence referendum.

When the Tory Chief Secretary to the Treasury, Greg Hands, discusses this provision in the Smith Commission, he keeps stressing the word "initially". This is just another way of saying that while the UK goverment promises not to penalise Scotland on the Monday, they reserve the right to rob Scotland's pay packet blind on Tuesday, Wednesday, Thursday, Friday, and on the weekend they're going to burgle our house. Greg thinks we don't realise how Westminster weasel words work.

Earlier this week we had the usual farce that passes for Scottish questions in the House of Commons, although English MPs Scoffing at Scotland would be a more accurate description. Just four out of the many MPs who spoke were Scottish MPs, and one of those was Tweedlemundell and the other Tweedlemurry. Remember when the UK government made a big deal out of how unfair it was that Scottish MPs might swing the balance on an English issue when England's representatives were pretty evenly divided? English

MPs dominating Scottish issues is the UK government's usual means of operation. It's a feature not a bug, no matter how much it bugs Scotland's voters.

The SNP moved a motion that would commit the UK government to the promises it made to the Smith Commission, that there should be no detriment to the Scottish budget as a result of the Scotland Act. The Tories came out of the woodwork of the Commons bars and voted against. Meanwhile Labour employed its usual Tory resisting tactics and bravely abstained again.

Labour abstains while the Tories slash Scotland's budget and rip up the Smith Commission, then they tell Scottish voters that we must pay a Better Together tax to make up the shortfall that Labour did nothing to forestall. The cuts to their budgets faced by Scottish local authorities are all the fault of the evil SNP. Labour is the guy who blames the first aider for not being quick enough with the bandages while ignoring the mad axeman who's chopping people's legs off. Actually it's worse than that. Labour connives with the mad axeman, because they'd far rather blame the SNP than oppose the Tories. Labour and the Tories are playing the same mendacious game.

There's no profit for Scotland in reaching an agreement with a duplicitous government in Westminster which views the Scotland Act as a means to screw us over. There's no profit in appeasing a Labour Party in Opposition that only opposes anything that's to Scotland's advantage. One of the greatest lessons from the civil rights campaigns of the twentieth century is that the first step to personal liberation is to stop cooperating with your own oppression. If Scotland's government consents to being robbed, then Scotland can't complain about it.

Let's not consent to being robbed. Let's not consent to being ripped off. Let's not consent to being lied to. The Scottish government should tell Westminster where they can stick their financial agreement. The Scottish electorate is sophisticated enough to know where the real blame lies.

6 February 2016

"No detriment", in real money, turns out to mean £7bn

The UK government has difficulty understanding the meaning of the phrase "no detriment". This was a key phrase in the Smith Commission report to which the UK government signed up, and having refused to acknowledge that the voters of Scotland upped their expectations with the pandafication of the Unionist parties in last May's Westminster elections, the Smith Commission remains the last official word in devolution. However Davie Cameron and the UK Treasury now want to redefine no detriment to mean £7 billion worth of detriment, and are upset that the Scottish government isn't detrimenting itself sufficiently. They want more mental detritus from Scotland.

I don't know about you, but I had always thought that the first rule of traps was that you don't advertise your trap with big signs saying TRAP all lit up in neon by yoonatic journalists. Now the UK government is upset that the Scottish government isn't obliging by walking into the trap. This is unfair, especially after the Wile E. Coyotes of the UK Treasury went to all the bother of painting a railway tunnel on a rock and getting a sign saying "Free Birdseed" from the ACME trap catalogue while they sat there on their rocket sled. And then that John Swinney just goes meep meep and runs off with the fiscal settlement while the express train of Scottish opinion flattens what's left of support for the Looney Yoons British government.

Having failed to get their trap to work on account of the fact that they'd forgotten that traps only work when the trappee doesn't know they're there, the UK government is now begging the Scottish government to meet them halfway. Instead of cutting the Scottish budget by £7 billion on top of the cuts that George Osborne is going to impose on us anyway, the UK Treasury will still cut the Scottish budget by £2.5 billion but will throw in a frayed Pokemon card and three pieces of bubblegum, one of which hasn't been chewed. It's still a trap, but with a small amount of stale confectionary as extra bait, followed by type 2 diabetes and a sugar crash.

The not so cunning plan of the UK government in its really-we-are-sincere commitment to further devolution was to offer the Scottish parliament a brand new shiny bicycle. Here take this bicycle, then you can cycle further into devolution than you ever thought possible, they said. Only the price of giving Scotland the bicycle was to cut Holyrood's legs off, then Westminster could tut that Scotland had all these lovely new powers but wasn't using them. What they're now attempting is to give Holyrood the bicycle and they're promising not to cut Holyrood's legs off, they're just going to break them in six places. This is what Westminster means by meeting Scotland halfway.

That's those Scots and their grievances, what are they like? This is the Unionist definition of grievance, which like the Unionist definition of no detriment, doesn't mean what everyone else thinks it means. In this instance grievance means that Scotland is opposing unfair Conservative policies that we didn't vote for and refusing to cut our fiscal throats in order to placate Tory backbenchers from Kent.

Scotland shouldn't be meeting Westminster half-way. The commitment to no detriment was all that was left after the watering down of devolution of the Smith Commission. Just about every other commitment that the Unionist parties made during the last days of the referendum has been wriggled out of, ignored or voted down. Scotland's MPs are excluded from voting on English issues, but English MPs dominate Scottish Questions. We still have control of traffic signs, but everything else gets a red light.

The stalling of the devo-deal came in the same week that scientists proved the theory of relativity with the discovery of gravity waves. The discovery came thanks to advances in the exploration of the cold distant depths of space, devoid of human life. There are two massive black holes locked in a cosmic dance sucking in all energy and matter until they destroy everything around them in a toxic burst of radioactivity. But enough about Labour and the Tories. Scotland can escape their orbit.

A government elected by the people of Scotland to defend and further the interests of Scotland cannot agree to a settlement which is detrimental to Scotland, no matter how much Westminster complains. The

Conservatives are convinced that the SNP is so desperate for extra powers for Holyrood that it will accept a deal giving extra powers that only damage and diminish Scotland's room for movement. But the only parties willing to damage Scotland's interests in pursuit of short-term political gain are the Unionist ones. If the Scotland Bill is detrimental to Scotland's interests, it's not a bill that Scotland wants or needs. Let the Coyote get caught in his own trap.

13 February 2016

Beware of Boris, the UK version of Trump

The UK media spent much of the weekend waiting to see whether the clownish Borish Johnson would squirt Davie Cameron in the face with his jokey English rose. The UK media is obsessed by the carefully constructed buffoonery of an egomaniac because he's the closest thing that the UK has to its very own Donald Trump. He's got the bad hair, the same overweening sense of entitlement, and has successfully pitched his careerism as character. Boris has devoted his public life to proving that if the fawning minions of the British press ever get fed up with the self-absorbed entitlement of an Etonian like Davie Cameron, other self-absorbed entitled Etonians are available.

Having invited a crowd of TV crews to his front door naturally the professional Pierrot obliged with a show of carefully constructed bumbling. After deep soul-searching about what would be best for his job prospects, he professed himself unconvinced by Davie's EU deal. I can't find it within me to support the prime minister, he rambled, because crikey obscure Classical reference, I've calculated that I have a better chance of getting his job, tousle hair harrumph, if I lead a successful Out campaign. Now watch me get stuck halfway down a zip wire waving the Union flag. Such larks.

In his article in the *Telegraph* explaining his decision to work for the furtherance of his career, Boris dismissed the possibility that Scotland which voted to remain in the EU would seek a fresh independence referendum if the rest of the UK voted to leave. "The evidence I have seen suggests that the Scots will vote on roughly the same lines as the English," opined Boris, leaving open the question of which evidence he'd seen. Reading articles in the *Telegraph* or the *Spectator* doesn't count as evidence of Scottish public opinion, as the only group less in touch with Scottish public opinion than Etonian politicians is the right-wing Scottish media commentariat, the ones who keep telling us that Labour is about to recover, or that Ruth Davidson is the most popular politician in Scotland since Robert the Bruce.

The dubious charms of Boris might enjoy a certain attraction in parts of the UK, in the same way that bluebottles are attracted to flypaper, but Scotland is thankfully immune. Nevertheless for the next four months we'll be getting intense media coverage of what Boris thinks about the free movement of people who didn't go to Eton, the single currency, and how he's now besties with Nigel Farage and George Galloway. There hasn't been such an unappealing pantomime combo since the Krankies teamed up with John Barrowman.

Project Eurofear is already well under way. Out supporting Iain Duncan Smith, who thinks that human decency is an imposition from Brussels that the UK could well do without, made a speech over the weekend warning that if Britain remains in the

EU it would be at risk of a Paris-style terrorist attack. Presumably IDS believes that the British citizens who became suicide bombers on the London Tube would have been deterred if only it wasn't for the Common Agricultural Policy. There hasn't been such a stupidly offensive pronouncement from a Tory politician since the last time IDS opened his uncaring gob.

Meanwhile Michael Gove, the Aberdonian who couldn't get elected in Aberdeen because his style of politics are electoral suicide in Scotland and had to run off south to find a safe seat in Toryshire, has announced that he's in favour of Brexit because he thinks the fundamental principle in politics is that a country should be able to elect who governs it. No really, he actually said that. Mikey fled from Scotland in order to escape being flattened by the crushing weight of his own irony overload.

For Scotland, the EU referendum is somewhat like the Royal Wedding. There will be wall-to-wall coverage of the event on the telly, while reporters rush up and down the country desperately trying to find someone who cares. In a Tory civil war you wish that both sides could lose.

Scotland now faces months of having our political agenda being dominated by a question that none of our main political parties – not even it seems the Scottish Tories – are particularly interested in, a question that the Scottish electorate have long since considered settled. Our own parliamentary elections will be dominated by a non-question which gives huge publicity to the odious UKIP, meaning there's a very real risk that Scotland might be faced with some

UKIP MSPs for the very first time. We can only hope that it will split the Tory vote.

And it's all because the Tory Party in England wants to settle an issue that's been tearing it apart for decades. While the rest of the continent wants to tackle issues like the refugee crisis provoked by the war in Syria, the UK Tories are obsessed by the fact that a small number of EU citizens residing in the UK are sending child benefit to their families abroad. And these, let's not forget, are the British politicians who insisted that Scotland was parochial and provincial for wanting to consider the question of whether Scotland requires Westminster to mediate between us and the rest of the world.

The EU referendum will only serve to deepen the political chasm that has opened up between Scotland and the rest of the UK over the past decades. While the Remain and the Leave campaigns compete to outdo one another in scare stories and threats, Scotland will look on from the sidelines, constantly reminded that decisions made in Scotland count for little or nothing in the UK. So much for the promise that only a No vote in the independence referendum would secure Scotland's place in the EU. So much for the assertion that Scotland's voice was valued and important.

It doesn't matter to the UK establishment whether you're a Yes voter or a No voter, to them we're all just wee Jimmy Krankies to be patronised and ignored. While the UK establishment tears itself apart over Europe, they've torn up the Smith Agreement and Scotland is left without the settlement we were promised. The only good thing likely to come out of this entire sorry process from Scotland's point of view is that another tranche of people who voted No to independence realise that the British establishment sold them a lie.

24 February 2016

Tories are the Donald Trumps
of Scottish politics

The Tories are the Donald Trumps of Scottish politics: they're a bit of an embarrassment, no one will
admit to voting for them, and everyone wishes they'd
go away. It's the Scottish Tory Party conference this
weekend, although if you're under the age of seventy
you could be forgiven for not noticing. The annual
gathering of Scottish Tories is the only party conference in Scotland where there's a resuscitation
team and a zimmer frame hire shop on hand. The
conference will be attended by the usual Tory lob-
byists, arms industry shills, private medicine companies, hedge funds, the Vampire Defence League, and
those shops which sell trousers with the waistband
up to your chest.

It's a peculiar reality of Scottish public life that we
have more Conservative journalists than Conservative
politicians, by quite some considerable margin. If it
wasn't for the attendance of a suspiciously non-critical
press at the Tory Party conference it could quite easily
be held in the Bide-A-Wee Retirement Shed for crusty
old imperialists, squeezed in between a rusty lawn-
mower with a broken blade and a bottle of paraquat.

These are the people who constantly tell us that
the Scottish public loves Ruthie. No. No, we really

don't. And they are always telling us that the Scottish Tories are about to make an electoral breakthrough and how the SNP popularity has peaked thanks to the Ruthie Warrior Princess astride her tank turret and her faithful sidekick Mundanielle. But there's as much chance of that happening as there is of Channel 5 getting through an evening's programming without any poverty porn.

On Friday, Defence Secretary Michael Fallon announced to the conference that the UK government is determined to go ahead and spend an extra £640 million on the renewal of Trident missiles, on top of the squillions that have already been set aside. The UK government can't find the money for a free helpline for benefits claimants, they can't find the money to pay junior doctors, they can't find many tax payments from Google, but they can find the money to spend on an offensive weapon system that has the potential to evaporate half the planet.

That's what they mean when they say Britain punches above its weight. They mean death, destruction, destroying and devastation. They mean that the UK is the Pentagon's go-to guy when it needs a fig leaf of internationalisation as a cover. They don't mean that the UK sets the gold standard in kindness and consideration. Punching above our weight is a violent metaphor for a violent state.

The government is pledging the money even before MPs have had a chance to debate Trident renewal in the House of Commons. Fallon announces that the replacement to Trident is already under way without even the fig leaf of democratic scrutiny. Announcing it in Scotland is another example of the Tory government's respect agenda for Scotland. That's respect in the sense that two fingers is a respectful salute. It's not just that the Tories don't give a toss about Scottish public opinion, they enjoy making a show of not giving a toss. This is what Scotland voted for when it voted against independence. We voted for smug Tories to rub our noses in our powerlessness.

There's no moral, logical or coherent argument for Trident or its replacement. Not that that stops some in the Labour Party from trying. Just think of the jobs, say some in Labour and some trade unions. Just think of Jackie Baillie's opportunities for getting on the telly to say just think of the jobs. Just think of Kezia Dugdale's opportunities for claiming that renewing Trident is the way to get rid of it.

Treating Trident like a job creation scheme is like arguing that the health service shouldn't supply drug addicts with methadone because it puts drug dealers out of work. If we'd listened to that argument then putting children up chimneys would still be legal. The simple fact of the matter is that if your job depends on maintaining a weapons system that can blow up the entire country, if it's a weapon of mass destruction whose use is immoral and an obscenity, then you're in the wrong job.

Yesterday Davie Cameron came and made some more threats, this time about leaving the EU. The Tory Party conference clapped politely and nodded in agreement. At least those of them who hadn't nodded off. In a normal universe, the Scottish Tories would be an irrelevant fringe party, UKIP latte as opposed to the Faragistas' full-on frothy cappuccino. There would be no need for anyone except diehard politics geeks to pay them the slightest bit of notice. But this party of superannuated fringe players is actually our government thanks to their support south of the border.

Tories cut Scotland's budget. Tories take your benefits. Tories foist nuclear warheads on us. Tories threaten to tear us out of the EU. Tories threaten the future of the NHS. Tories slash your public services then tell you to clean for the Queen. Those aren't threats, those are realities of Scottish life.

Until we arrive in a Scotland where the conference of a fringe party can be safely ignored like the contents of your shed, there's going to be an independence movement. And thanks to the Tories, one day, sooner than you might think, that independence movement is going to win.

5 March 2016

The twentieth century Fox
denies took place

Liam Fox is a former Tory defence secretary and now a leading proponent of the view that it's terribly unfair that a country has its laws made for it by politicians whom it doesn't elect and can't throw out of office. Except, of course, when that country is Scotland and the politicians are Tories like Liam. Liam's belief in the value of national sovereignty begins and ends with the Westminster parliament.

Just a few days ago, Liam was urging the public not to be bullied by the SNP into voting for EU membership. A man who represents a party that the Scottish electorate rejected comprehensively, and yet that same party slashes the benefits of the Scottish poor while rewarding the rich, has no right to complain about being bullied. But then self-awareness, or indeed basic human decency, was never a strong point of a Scottish Conservative who's only an MP in the first place because he had to run away down south to find people to vote for him.

This week, the man who resigned office after he was unable to bury his friendship with Adam Werritty announced that the UK is one of the few EU countries that doesn't need to bury its twentieth-century history. Perhaps Liam specified the twentieth century because the UK's crimes prior to the twentieth century are too numerous to list in a short article, including the world's most thorough genocide, the near total wiping out of the entire native population of Tasmania.

But British twentieth-century history has been nothing but glorious hasn't it. Not like those Germans, the ones you can't mention the war in front of. That would be the Germans who teach their children about their country's past crimes so that future generations won't repeat the mistakes of the past. British school children don't get taught about the British carpet bombing of the historic German city of Dresden in the final months of the war when German collapse was imminent. The bombing killed 25,000 civilians, and didn't do anything to bring about an earlier end to a war that Germany had already lost.

The British haven't ever committed war crimes. It's blasphemous to suggest that they might have in the state sponsored glorification of all things military that dominates the UK these days. So let's not mention the torture and castration faced by anti-colonialists in Kenya, or the concentration camps into which Afrikaners and Black South Africans were herded during the Boer War. During the Mau Mau uprising against British rule in Kenya, the British hanged over 1000 Kenyans, many more than the French executed in their war in Algeria.

But those were wars. It was during peacetime that the French deported an indigenous people and destroyed their Pacific island homeland with nuclear testing. The British would never do anything like that.

Oh no. Except of course they did exactly that. Just ask the Native Australian tribe of Maralinga, whose most sacred Dreamtime site was destroyed by British nuclear testing. It was the equivalent of packing St Paul's Cathedral with Semtex. Or ask the inhabitants of the Chagos Islands, who were packed off to Mauritius on a cargo boat and summarily dumped on the quayside because the UK had leased their islands to the USA for an airbase.

Ask the people of the Indian city of Amritsar, the holy city of the Sikhs. In 1919, fearing insurrection, British army soldiers fired on unarmed civilians hemmed in in an enclosed space who had gathered to celebrate a religious festival, killing 379 according to the official account. Unofficial accounts put the true number of those killed far higher. Colonel Reginald Dyer, the commanding officer who gave the order to fire on unarmed civilians, was lauded as a hero by Conservative politicians of the day.

Although Dyer was eventually forced to retire from the army following an official enquiry, he was awarded £26,000 (about £1 million in today's money) from a fund set up by the conservative *Morning Post* newspaper, which later merged with the *Telegraph*. After a long campaign, families of the victims of the massacre were finally awarded compensation from the British government. They got £37.50 each, equivalent to about £1000 in today's money.

Then there's the British role in Ireland, in Iraq, in Palestine, Suez, Malaya and in pretty much every conflict in the twentieth century. The only time that the UK was unequivocally the good guys was when

Britain was up against your actual Nazis. Saying that the UK's role in history is less morally reprehensible than Hitler's or Stalin's isn't much of a boast.

The only reason that people like Liam can claim that the UK doesn't need to bury any of its twentieth-century history is because the nasty parts of the UK's recent past have been comprehensively airbrushed by the supine British media out of public consciousness. The British history that people like Liam celebrate bears as much relation to reality as the Photoshopped glam shots of a model with an eating disorder bear to the average woman.

But you don't need to trawl through recent history in order to find shameful episodes in which the British government is complicit. British shamefulness is going on right now, right here, and the Conservative government that Liam Fox supports is directly responsible for it.

There's a litany of shame in a street near you. This is one of the most unequal countries in Europe, where the bosses pay themselves obscene wages while workers struggle to make ends meet. People who work in supermarkets can't afford to shop there but the directors cream off millions. Food banks rise along with the numbers whose access to social security is cut by box ticking workers with quotas of shame to fill or they'll join the ranks of the sanctioned. Affordable housing is a dream fewer can attain. Homelessness soars, and Liam Fox's Tory colleagues claim sleeping rough is a lifestyle choice. Having been a leading player in the wars that have provoked the biggest refugee crisis since WW2, the UK refuses to accept those refugees.

Britain's modern international reputation is one of greed, selfishness and insularity. And that's due in no small measure to the self-satisfied preening of the myopic Liam Fox with his one-sided view of history. He wants out of the EU so Britain can glory in its shameful isolation.

9 March 2016

Osborne Hood and his merry menace

On Monday we were all invited to be offended at the news that *Top Gear*'s new presenters had filmed a stunt near the Cenotaph in London. It was, we were told, grossly offensive to the dead. This is the UK, where the sensibilities of those long dead count for far more than those who are still alive and scraping a meagre living. The same commentators who rush to condemn the presenters of *Top Gear*, the televisual version of motorised trolling, look the other way when the targets are disabled people in Britain. We live under a government which believes that if a person is unable to go to the toilet unassisted, if they can't dress themselves without help, then the best way to help them is to leave them lying naked in their own filth. That'll teach them.

Today when Chancellor of the Exchequer George Osborne presents his budget to the House of Commons he is expected to announce yet further reductions in the amount paid in social security to the poorest and most vulnerable. Many of those affected by the UK government's £1.2 billion assault on the social security payments made to disabled people are ex-servicemen and women. What George Osborne is doing is a far greater insult to the memory of the war dead than any stupid wee stunt by Matt LeBlanc in a souped-up motor.

The glorious dead thought they were fighting and laying down their lives to make Britain a country which cared for the sick and the poor. What they actually died for was a country that won't even look after those who were maimed in its service, never mind people who were born with a disability or who became ill in later life. The rich boys of the Tory cabinet think that the route out of poverty is best achieved by slashing the support received by the poor. It's a bit like claiming that you're more likely to climb a ladder after most of the rungs have been removed, and in this case that ladder was to be used by people who had mobility problems to begin with.

What tranforms George Osborne's raid on the care budgets of the most vulnerable from merely disgusting to maliciously malign is that the reason for the cut is to fund a tax break for the better-off. For this government it's more of a priority that Jocasta and Sebastian can afford a proper Aga for the kitchen of their weekend country cottage in the Cotswalds and be spared the social disgrace of dinner parties around an inferior range than it is for a person with disabilities to get help with cooking a hot meal. George Osborne is Robin Hood in reverse, stealing from the poor to give to the rich.

George is only perpetuating a pattern established by the last Labour government, the one which was infamously very relaxed about people getting seriously rich. According to an analysis by the charity Oxfam, since the year 2000 the richest one per cent of people in Britain, people who are already millionaires, have seen their net wealth increase by over £1 trillion. By 2015 the top one per cent in the UK were worth an average of £3.7 million each, an increase of £1.5 million on the year 2000. That represents over a quarter of the increase in national wealth over the past fifteen years. The bottom half of the population received just seven per cent of the increase in national wealth. The wealth of the UK is hoovered up by the rich with the voracity of a cocaine addict's nose.

Today the Chancellor is expected to announce that he's raising the tax thresholds for the better-paid, so that those who can already afford to live comfortably can enjoy life even more. It's the poorest who will pay for it. It's the trickle down economy. This is how we're better together in this UK, that's the pooling and sharing that Gordie Broon went on about. We pool our resources so the rich can take all the shares, and the only thing that trickles down is the rain on the heads of the homeless. But according to unelected Tory minister Susan Williams, who was given a peerage after the voters rejected her, sleeping rough is a lifestyle choice.

Last weekend Osborne told Andrew Marr on the BBC that he needed to find additional savings equivalent to 50p in every £100 the government spends by the end of the decade. Those savings won't be coming out of the pockets of the top one per cent. If previous budgets are anything to go by, Osborne's speech today will be characterised by headline announcements that look glossy and shiny, but which fall apart more quickly than Jackie Baillie's calculations on the back of a Labour leaflet.

Analyses show that Britain's GDP will be £18 billion lower than predicted this year; this budget is going to be more severe in order to make up the shortfall. You can be certain that it won't be the Aga buyers of the Cotswalds who're going to pay for it. Whatever else happens in this year's budget we can be sure that Osborne's interventions on behalf of the poor will be as welcome as a lard soaked bridie at a vegan wedding, and every bit as unhealthy.

As Osborne was schmoozing with the BBC, putting lipstick on the pig of a budget after it had been out on a date with Davie, the SNP Party conference was going on in Glasgow. The highlight of the weekend was Nicola Sturgeon's announcement that if elected the SNP will spend the next few years making the case for independence, to convert the undecided to the independence cause. A few more budgets from Osborne and the SNP won't need to do much of anything to make a case. The Conservatives are making that case for us, while Labour thinks that opposition means abstaining.

With every passing day of a majority Conservative government the true horrors of the UK are being revealed in all their malicious greed. We're living in the final days of the Union, it's eating itself with its own avarice and cruelty.

16 March 2016

Scots language under attack from *Daily Mail* — again

Well here we go again. This week the *Daily Mail* graced us with a full page of ignorant nonsense about the Scots language, or more exactly, what at least one of its prominent fanboys promoted on Twitter as the truth about the pretend slang that you're paying for with your taxes. According to the *Mail*, which has never been noted for allowing reality to get in the way of a venting a prejudice, the SNP government has embarked upon a madcap mission to promote the "Scots language". The phrase Scots language is helpfully given in scare quotes in order that the sensitivities of *Daily Mail* readers might be spared from dangerous separatism.

The article is a ridiculous confection of ragbag prejudices and stereotypes about the Scots language, written by a person whose familiarity with the linguistic and academic work on the language is less than the sympathy expressed for refugees in a typical *Daily Mail* editorial. Anyone who says there is no such thing as the Scots language, merely a ragbag collection of words and phrases, is as good as admitting that they have no clue what they're writing about and that they haven't even bothered to do the most basic of research. Linguists who have published papers and monographs on Scots phonology and syntax will be relieved that a journalist on the *Daily Mail* has put them to rights.

The author of the piece then went on to cite the use of the construction "had went" as an example of bad grammar masquerading as Scots when in fact it's a dialectal construction found in English and the citation given was used in a context which was clearly English-speaking. The Scots version is of course "had gaed". The only connection this has to the status or non-status of Scots as a language is the author's linguistic prejudice.

The main misrepresentations in the article are threefold, and all are typical of a certain brand of Scottish Unionist who refuses to admit that there is any cultural distinctiveness about Scotland.

Firstly there is the notion that the drive to create a standardised literary variety of Scots is a creature of the SNP government. The truth is that Scots has a long history of attempts at standardisation, dating back to the embryonic standard Scots of the sixteenth century, through Hugh MacDiarmid's attempts to create a non-dialectal Scots literary language in the early twentieth century. The Scottish government of today is legally obliged to support and promote the Scots language, not because of the SNP, but because the UK government listed Scots as one of the regional languages of the UK when it signed up to the European Charter for Regional or Minority Languages in 2000, long before the SNP got a sniff of power in Holyrood. Signing up to the charter obliges a government to protect and foster the languages it listed. Scots language versions of Scottish govern-ment websites exist because of the Labour Party, not the SNP. But that uncomfortable truth doesn't suit the Unionist narrative.

Secondly there is the belief that standard literary Scots is uniquely artificial, when in fact all stand-ardised literary languages are, almost by definition, artificial creations. Someone sat down and invented words or expanded the sense of existing words to cover new concepts. That's how all languages achieve standardisation. Writers and language activ-ists sit down and develop words for new concepts, or extend the meaning of existing words.

In the article words like wabsite for website were criticised as being pretend words when it's merely an example of calquing or loan translation. Calquing is a recognised technique for expanding the vocabu-lary of a language. Promotors of standardised Scots take existing Scots words and use them in new ways; that's not pretendy or artificial. The critics of Scots insist that it's not a language because it doesn't have words for certain concepts, then when those words are provided they decry them as invented.

There are actually some existing standard languages which contain entirely invented words. Estonian was standardised in the nineteenth century and includes words like *kolp* (skull), or *liibuma* (to cling), words which were invented out of nothing by the Estonian language activist Johannes Aavik. And then of course standard English contains words like saw-bones and flummox, invented by Charles Dickens, or chortle, snark and portmanteau, all coined by Lewis

Carroll. Some of these words have even appeared in the pages of Unionist tabloids without anyone getting hysterical about pretendy artificiality.

Thirdly there is the peculiar belief that promotion of Scots, or indeed Gaelic, means that proficiency in English is damaged as a result. This is a notion that goes all the way back to the Victorian belief that there was only so much space in the brain for language, and filling it up with a "useless" language like Scots or Gaelic meant less space for English. There is not a shred of scientific support for this belief, in fact the opposite is true. Educating Scots-speaking children bilingually in Scots and English will only improve the quality of their Scots and their English.

For a certain strain of Unionist, the Scots language doesn't exist, and when it is presented to them it's nothing more than an example of nationalist grievance. The real grievance here is the Unionist grievance that Scottish people are increasingly less tolerant of Unionist arrogance and ignorance dressed up as erudition, and we're going to keep calling them out on their Cringe.

19 March 2016

Why SNP mustn't lose any ground in the fight for a second independence referendum

It's not long now until the Scottish parliamentary elections, and it's growing ever more apparent that we need to ensure the election of another majority SNP government. The only way that we can be certain of having a second independence referendum, and even more importantly winning it, is if we keep the momentum going. If the SNP come out of this coming election with fewer seats than before, then that momentum is lost and we put the entire independence movement at risk.

Personally I feel caught between a rock and a hard place here, since I'm going to have to abstain in the constituency vote. There's a lot of talk and disagreement about who to give your list vote to, but some of us don't have anyone to give our constituency vote to. The only pro-independence candidate in the constituency where I live is the local SNP MSP. Sadly he is to lesbian and gay rights as King Herod is to kindergartens, and since sometime over the course of the next Scottish parliament I plan to marry an American, I'd be a whole lot more comfortable if I had an MSP who respected our right to wed if I have to contact him for assistance in dealing with the complexities of immigration law and getting my new husband into the country on a permanent footing. I'd rather not have a local constituency MSP who feels strongly that his god calls gay people to celibacy, because I feel every bit as strongly that my civil and human rights ought not to be a matter of his religious beliefs.

That leaves the list vote. I've got a lot of time for the Greens and would still give a list vote to them if I lived in the region where one of my best friends is standing for them, because he's one of the good guys. There's a great deal of what RISE says that makes sense and is appealing, and it would be great to see young and passionate voices like Cat Boyd get a platform in the Scottish parliament. But the truth is that it's only with another SNP majority government that we can keep independence at the forefront of Scottish political debate. So my second vote will be going to the SNP.

I am not convinced by arguments that you can vote tactically in the list. It's a system designed to ensure proportionality in the outcome, so if there's an absolute majority for the SNP in my region, then an absolute majority of the MSPs returned will be SNP. Thankfully those who have nineteenth-century views on the rights of lesbian and gay people are few and far between.

There is only one issue in Scottish politics more important than ensuring that we have a second independence referendum, and that's ensuring that we win the referendum when it happens. Only a second majority SNP government in May can guarantee that

Scotland stays on track for its eventual date with destiny. They might not be the most radical government in Scottish history, they're certainly open to criticism on a number of grounds, but they have proven themselves to be a competent government which by and large makes the best of the poor hand dealt to it by the Westminster parliament and the Tory Treasury.

However in one area the SNP have excelled themselves and surpassed all expectations. The single greatest achievement of the SNP has been to normalise the idea of independence and not only to bring it squarely into the mainstream of Scottish political discourse, but to make it the single most important question in Scottish politics. The SNP have changed the idea of independence from a romantic dream held by a few into something that most consider to be an inevitability. It's no longer a question of if Scotland should become independent, but of when. But that's only going to remain the case as long as we have a majority SNP government and as long as the SNP are seen as the winners in Scottish politics.

If the SNP are returned with fewer seats than they got in 2011, even if there is still a pro-independence majority thanks to Greens and RISE MSPs, there's only going to be one narrative in Scotland's overwhelmingly Unionist media. That will be the story of how the voters of Scotland have punished the Scottish government for holding the independence referendum and how the result is proof that a second referendum is not wanted. It will all be accompanied with exhultant crowing at the supposed downfall of nationalism, and the battered shreds of the Unionist parties will be garlanded as the triumphant victors, even if they've lost votes and lost seats. Cue a nauseating series of articles hailing Ruth Davidson as the saviour of the Union.

There's no balance or fairness in Scotland's media landscape. Any talk of a Unionist victory under such circumstances would of course be a complete fiction, but when has a lack of truth ever stopped Scotland's Unionist establishment from presenting their fantasies as fact? Despite all our talk of diversity, all our efforts to make the independence movement a broad church, the media identifies the cause of independence with the SNP, and any reversal of fortunes for that party will be presented as a reversal of fortunes for Scotland's progress to self-determination and statehood. That might not be fair, but it's the brutal reality.

Only with a second majority for the SNP will Scotland continue on its slow but steady progress to independence. Only with a second majority for the SNP can we persuade most people that a Scottish government can be quietly competent. And it's only with a second majority for the SNP that we can be certain that if there is a change in circumstances that a bill for a second independence referendum will be brought forward and won't be blocked by the Unionists.

Since these elections are being conducted under the shadow of the Conservatives' EU referendum, the stakes are very high indeed. We need an SNP majority to ensure that Scotland's voice isn't lost amongst the screams from the Tories.

20 April 2016

Roll on the day when Scotland can wave goodbye to the royals

This week, our unelected head of state turned ninety, and there was an orgy of sycophancy in the media which made the mediaeval writers of the lives of saints seem a tad hypercritical. It was hugely over the top for a woman whose greatest achievement, if we're being honest, is still being alive at the age of ninety. Although it is certainly the case that she is successfully keeping Prince Charles off the throne, and for that alone we must be grateful. Other rich aristos who know the Queen claim that she does have an achievement: she can do an accurate rendition of an Aberdeen accent. Which is a bit like someone who doesn't speak French claiming that someone else speaks French fluently. Mocking Scottish people isn't exactly the best way to worm your way into our affections.

Allegedly she works really hard, and this would be true, as long as you define hard work as walking very short distances while waving at the lower orders and receiving the adulation of an uncritical press. The only labour she's ever known was when she was giving birth to four children who have equally failed to do anything constructive. Except Charles of course, who has a full-time job writing crank letters to cabinet ministers. It says a lot about the sickness at the heart of the British constitution that the cabinet ministers have to reply to him, instead of filing his missives in the bin along with the other communiciations that they receive written in crayon.

If you were to believe the hype, the Queen is not only universally adored, but in her spare time, which she doesn't have much of what with all those walkabouts and waving at plebs, she turns water into wine and cures leprosy with the touch of her gloved hand. This is of course when she's not walking on water and exhibiting a wisdom that makes King Solomon seem like a bit of a dummy. We were told it was a wonderful time for the royals and the country as a whole and that joyful celebrations were the order of the day. Prince Harry got rat-faced and cavorted naked through the grounds of Buckingham Palace with a random model, and then someone told him it was his gran's birthday.

The Queen's legion of sycophants are so blindly loyal that she could trample one of them with a horse and they'd lie there broken and bleeding but still gushing about how marvellous she was. Although admittedly if she was to charge at Nicholas Witchell and run him over with the royal coach she would probably gain quite a few fans amongst republicans too.

There's little data to go on, but I get the impression that republican sentiment is a lot stronger in Scotland than elsewhere in the UK. Unlike the rest of this so-called United Kingdom, no one organises street parties to celebrate royal occasions. Instead we organise raves in parks which are explictly anti-monarchist and spend the day raising eyebrows and harrumphing at the sycophantic royalist excesses of a media that seems to be bent on enforcing a celebration of monarchy with no basis in reality instead of reflecting the real lack of interest that does exist. Being Scottish during a royal-fest is a bit like being a wean upset that they're going on holiday to a cold and damp Saltcoats while their mammy yells at them that they'd bloody better enjoy themself.

Yet the enforced gorging on bunting, bool-moothed minor aristos you've never heard of, and gushing platitudes is self-defeating. All it produces is increasing resentment at being told what to think and feel by an unthinking and unfeeling media. It puts into high relief that our media is not a mirror to this land but a propaganda movie directed by someone else far away. And they're missing a trick, when the BBC is about to embark upon yet another hagiographic inane celebration of the non-achievements of a well-born non-entity, it's the only time that people north of the border would actually welcome the continuity announcer saying, "Except for viewers in Scotland, who'll be getting indoor bowling from Coatbridge presented by Dougie Donnelly."

As far as the royal family and Scotland are concerned, less is more. The more they're stuck into our faces, the more we resent them. The royal family symbolises a British establishment that treats Scotland as a landed estate, a country that's a possession. They come to Scotland once or twice a year to stay in a castle and shoot things, they know nothing about our lives, and then have the gall to claim to the world that they represent us.

The disconnect between Scotland and the rest of the UK is writ large in the royal family. There's no chance of ever getting a republic while we're a part of the UK. In the UK there is only ever going to be compulsory bunting and Nicholas Witchell's sycophantic commentary. We're stuck with them until we get independence, and then we might get a parliament that will allow us to decide whether we want a monarch.

23 April 2016

You can vote for playtime power or a grown-up country

The Scottish election isn't until tomorrow, and the howls, wails and renting of garments has already started in a Unionist camp that is bracing itself for another defeat. The Westminions are getting their SNPbad in early, mind you, they never really stopped.

Over in the *Times*, BBC presenter the windswept but not really interesting Neil Oliver referred to the campaign for Scottish independence as a hate-fest. Scotland is a howling morass of vileness apparently. Neil is upset because he didn't expect to find himself in this position, a historian on the wrong side of history.

Usually what happens in independence campaigns is states of emergency, internment camps, extrajudicial deaths, bombings, and violence. Scotland had none of that, to the great and lasting credit of both the Yes and the No sides in the debate. Yet someone threw an egg at Jim Murphy, and this counts as a hate-fest. Still, Neil is well qualified as a Westminster apologist, what with him presenting all those archaeology programmes and the UK being the ruins of an ancient empire.

The objective truth is that Scotland is a model to the world about how to handle the issue of potential independence. The lack of violence in the Scottish independence campaign is a testament to the great political maturity of Scottish people and to our commitment to democracy. The Scottish process was held up in admiration in other nations around the world. We deserve a collective pat on the back. Yet people like Neil Oliver go on about hate-fests oblivious to the fact that the only violence on display during the independence referendum campaign was on a par with that seen during any election campaign, and with the exception of an egg it all came from the Unionist side.

Some others have been complaining that pro-independence satirists don't attack the most dominant party in Scotland. What sort of satire is that, they ask, in what is really a plea for pro-independence supporters to make jokes at the expense of the independence side because Unionists lack the wit to do so with any great success. No matter how many heartfelt articles the Unionist apologists write for the papers telling us how awful the SNP is, no matter how often or how hysterically they scream about the badness that lurks at the heart of pro-independence parties, they gain no traction with the voters.

It's a tough gig, being a Unionist opinion former and no one comes round to your opinions. Instead they're reduced to complaining that independence supporters aren't doing their job for them. Why aren't you attacking the SNP eh? Eh? They're the Scottish establishment, not us, poor wee harmless Unionists that we are. It's the SNP that ought to be the target for your witty barbs and jibes and cartoons featuring goldfish. What they're really saying is dear God please give us a break, do our job for us because we're failing miserably. It's a cry for help. They need all the help they can get, because certain Unionist cartoonists in supposedly leftish British newspapers think that satire is mushing up Nicola Sturgeon's face.

The only part of the Unionist ruminator complaint that is correct is that it is indeed the job of the satirist to attack and make fun of the powerful, but that's exactly what pro-independence satirists do and their targets are spot on. That's because the dominant and most powerful political parties in Scotland are still the Conservative Party and the Labour Party.

It doesn't matter that the voters of Scotland have numerically turned the representatives of these parties into pandas. These are pandas that are not confined to a zoo. They're confined to Westminster, which admittedly can be difficult to distinguish from a zoo. However they're still the most powerful parties in Scotland, not the SNP, and certainly not the broader independence movement.

It's a Unionist party that tells Scotland if it's going to war. It's a Unionist party that imposes nuclear weapons on Scotland despite the fact our own elected representatives are overwhelmingly opposed. It's a Unionist party that sets Scotland's budget and which decides what the Scottish parliament does or does not have powers over. And it's going to be a Unionist party that does that irrespective of how much support it gets in Scotland.

The SNP is the biggest party inside the little play-pen of Scottish politics, but it's still a Unionist party that guards the bars of the pen and keeps us in our place. It's still a Unionist party that tells us what toys we can play with. It's still a Unionist party that tells us when it's time to go to bed. It's still a Unionist party that tells us what we can watch on the telly.

We're currently in a situation where the most powerful political party in Scotland, the party that determines your pension, your benefits, your retirement age, is a party that receives a mere 14.8 per cent of the popular vote and is blessed with a single MP who, when you look at him in poor light could easily be mistaken for Paddington Bear. We're controlled and dominated by parties that we don't vote for, yet if you're a Scottish satirist you're supposed to ignore that glaring iniquity and concentrate your fire on the goings-on within the little playpen.

Ever since I started writing and blogging about Scottish politics, I've refrained from attacking the SNP, the Greens or the socialist parties. My goal is independence, and I've never made any secret about that. We live in a country whose media is ridiculously skewed and unbalanced. *The National* is the only daily newspaper that supports a constitutional settlement which has the backing of around half the Scottish population, and it's a recent development. Scotland's media landscape is overwhelmingly Unionist, and if the massed forces of Scotland's professional Unionist media are not capable of successfully satirising the independence movement on their own, that's entirely down to their own inadequacies. I'm not in the business of doing their job for them or supplying them with ammunition to make up for their own shortcomings.

We have a vote tomorrow. I'm going to vote for Scotland to be a grown-up and mature country, a country that takes responsibility for itself. I want to live in a Scotland that profits from its own successes, and deals with its own failures. The Unionists want a Scotland that is infantilised, that is kept in the play-pen while the big boys and girls that we can't control or influence make decisions on our behalf. There's going to be a lot more howling from the Unionists after tomorrow.

4 May 2016

Time for Labour to decide whose side they're on

The good news is that the Scottish parliament still has a majority of pro-independence MSPs. There's going to be another SNP Scottish government, for the third time in a row, and together with an increased representation from the Greens there is still a majority in Holyrood for pro-independence parties. With the demise of the Labour Party, the Scottish independence movement has now established itself as the only political force in Scotland which supports progressive, social democratic politics.

If you want to ensure that the NHS is safe, that we get rid of Trident, that there's land reform, protection of workers' rights, that we keep the Scottish education system with its commitment to free tuition, if you want to develop renewable energy and a sustainable reindustrialisation, if you want to retain jobs in Scotland, there's only one way to go. That's to support independence. The longer we remain a part of the UK, the more we put at risk all the things that Better Together assured us could only be safe if Scotland voted No.

The election was an object lesson in just how unusual and difficult it is for any party to obtain an absolute majority under the D'Hondt method of voting, although the SNP have done amazingly well for a party seeking a third term in government, especially given the absolute pasting they receive on a daily basis from an overwhelmingly Unionist media. Don't forget that in terms of the number of votes received, SNP support increased. Unfortunately for them, this time the voting system didn't work in their favour.

There's also the minor conciliation that having arrived at his count in a plumber's van, David Coburn and UKIP were flushed away. They failed to make any breakthrough in Scotland, which bodes well for the Scottish vote in next month's EU referendum.

The bad news is the large number of gains made by the Ruth Davidson for More Ruth Davidson Ruth Davidsonning the Bad SNP Ruth Davidson Party (Ruth Davidson Branch) and her legions of supporters in the Scottish media. The lesson for the Scottish Unionist media is that if you keep hyping one Unionist party leader after another, eventually one of them is going to deliver some victories. Ruthie is the toast of the Tories today, but she's going to have to do a lot more than scream SNPbad from the top of a tank if she wants to prove that she has any substance.

The devastation wrought upon the Labour Party benefitted the SNP in the West, but in the rest of the country the spoils went to the Don't Mention That We're Tories Party. Or at least they weren't mentioning that they were Tories before the election; they're positively crowing about it now. The Tories are now the second largest party in the parliament, and the major representatives of Scottish Unionism.

What the collapse of Labour means is that Scottish Unionism has now been clearly revealed in all its ugly glory. Unionism in Scotland means the destruction of the welfare state, the widening gulf of inequality, tax breaks for the rich, the entrenchment of the privileges of the better-off, the preservation of the landed estates, the renewal of Trident, and the evisceration of employment and social rights. The lesson that the Yes movement needs to take on board is that there is a significant segment of Scottish opinion which is so afraid of independence that they will put their trust in a party which openly threatens to privatise the state and destroy the social fabric of the very country that they claim they wish to preserve.

Labour are the big losers. They're a party which has lost its soul and lost its reason for being. A long time ago they ceased to be the workers' party and became the party of managing the workers' expectations on behalf of the bosses. They ceased to be the party of Scotland when they used devolution for their own short-term political gain. They tried to appeal to Yes supporters on the one side, and No voters on the other, and ended up appealing to neither. They're a party which has no point and no purpose. The demise of Labour isn't over yet. The local elections are only a year away and their last bastions in local government look set to fall too.

There's now a sharp divide in the Scottish political landscape between a progressive social democratic eco-friendly independence movement dedicated to increasing the powers of the Scottish parliament and the Scottish people, and a reactionary conservative

Unionism dedicated to preserving the privileges of the better-off and the British establishment.

It is now clearer than ever that the future and safety of our NHS, our public services, our employment rights, our civil rights, our education system, the removal of Trident, and the development of renewable energies go hand in hand with the progress of the independence movement. What's left of the Labour Party in Scotland needs to decide which side of the divide it stands on.

7 May 2016

Ulsterised? More like Catalonia in the rain

There's a new theme amongst Unionist commentators. You can't simultaneously go on decrying that Scotland is a one-party state while celebrating the supposed victory of the Vote Ruth Davidson Don't Mention the Tories Oh Look a Photo Op on a Buffalo Party, and so a different narrative to diminish and demean Scotland's independence supporters is required. Something with a hint of menace, and preferably carrying the implication that Scottish people are not in fact genetically programmed to make their own decisions after all, because as mere northern barbarians we require the good services of the British state to save us from ourselves.

Thankfully, as reliably as a Lib Dem lost deposit, a new slur has come along just in time. Scotland isn't a one-party state any more because Ruthie is the new champion of Union. It's worse than a one-party state. Scottish politics has now suffered full on Ulsterisation instead. You can tell that from the lamentable fact that if you poke your eyes out with a rusty knitting needle Nicola Sturgeon looks exactly like Gerry Adams, and Yes supporters preach a reactionary religious sectarianism and parade up and down high streets wearing bowler hats and sashes. Oh, wait.

The term, Unionist commentators faux innocently claim, refers to the fact that Scottish politics now revolve around the constitutional question. You know, like it hasn't been doing that for the past five years or more. The question of independence or union is the only show in town. No really, that's all there is to it. We're as honest as a Ruth Davidson photo op guv. It's an entirely neutral observation, we're just trying to be helpful. And if you believe that you probably also believe that *Reporting Scotland* really does present a fair, unbiased and totally representative picture of Scottish news and current affairs and it's perfectly normal for self-governing nations not to have their own public service broadcast channel. Oh look, there's a wee cute kitten, and now for the fitba.

The term Ulsterisation carries nasty overtones of an armed struggle, of sectarianism, of violence and death, discrimination and abuse. That's deliberate. It also carries with it implications that the positions of Unionists and independentistas are entrenched and generational and presumably also that the Unionist majority is set in stone. It is certainly not. Scottish Unionism is nowhere near as entrenched or as inherited as its Northern Irish equivalent. Scottish Unionism is weak, fragile and highly conditional. It's due to the weakness of their own position that Scottish Unionist commentators are forced to make facile comparisons with Northern Ireland in an attempt to bolster their own waning support. It only illustrates their own intellectual and moral bankruptcy. Scottish Unionism is dying. It has been brain-dead for quite a while now, as the recent claim of Ulsterisation of Scottish politics proves. The only Troubles in Scotland are the troubles of a discredited Unionist commentariat.

Unionism and independence are not sectarian positions in Scotland. The use of the term Ulsterisation is an attempt to suggest that there is a sectarian component to Scottish politics, that we vote from a religious or emotive belief instead of a considered view that a country is best governed by people who actually live in it. There is a sectarian taint to Scottish politics, but it is entirely confined to a small number on the more lunatic and screaming fringes of Unionism. Sectarianism in Scottish politics is a problem for Unionists, not for nationalists, although you'll wait in vain for any Unionist commentator to admit that. Their use of the term Ulsterisation merely reminds Scotland of the ugly outer edges of Unionism, that Scotland has a small number of Unionists who were born British, who live British, who vote British and who by God will die British. Which only goes to show that some people have got no ambition or imagination at all.

There are other countries that our not so clever-clever Unionists could have chosen for their comparison. Northern Ireland is not the only other place on this planet where politics revolve around a constitutional question. A far more accurate comparision would have been to say that Scottish politics are now characterised by Catalanisation. That's another European country where politics revolves entirely around the question of independence or union, and does so with sun, sand and sangria, not sectarianism, segregation and cries of no surrender.

They could have said that Scottish politics were now displaying Quebeckisation. This is also an accurate comparison as the Quebecois national dish is poutine, made of chips, cheese curd and gravy, and both Scots and Quebecois people are far more likely to have a debate about the future of their country over a plate of chips and a beer than they are to throw a petrol bomb while singing songs about Fenian blood.

But then Catalonia and Quebec are foreign nations, and Unionists don't do foreign. That means lifting your eyes beyond the confines of the British state and realising that there's a whole big world out there full of possibilities that are not constrained by Westminster. Besides, those comparisons lack the necessary overtones of atavistic violence and menace that Unionist commentators just love to impute to Scottish nationalism despite all the objective evidence showing that the real reactionary and violent atavism lies with the more extreme factions of Unionism.

Although the only people in Scotland to have been charged with politically motivated violence, abuse or harrassment have been Unionists whose victims have been independence supporters, the Unionist media is determined to preserve its narrative that there is a violent and racist undercurrent to the demand for Scottish self-determination. Unionists guilty of violence and abuse are individuals acting on their own, they're just aberrations that tell us nothing about Unionism and how very dare you imply that mainstream Unionists have anything to do with them. However independence supporters guilty of far less serious offences are symptomatic of the independence movement as a whole and Nicola Sturgeon must condemn them.

The Ulsterisation jibe is the latest Unionist manifestation of media attempts to demonise the independence campaign and to dissuade Scots from engaging with it. It tells people to get back into their box because opening the box might lead to violence and sectarian strife. It adds nothing to the understanding of where Scotland is or where it is going, and it won't succeed in putting a stop to the independence campaign. All it does is to show that those commentators who use it disqualify themselves from having any meaningful contribution to the debate about Northern Ireland or the debate about Scotland.

11 May 2016

It's time for our MSPs to swear a new oath

This week, following the elections that according to the Unionist press the Ruth Davidson Look at Me I'm Riding a Buffalo Whoo Hoo Ruth Davidson Party won by coming a very distant second, Scotland's new MSPs were sworn in to the parliament that represents the democratic will of the Scottish people. You might think that Scottish MSPs swearing an oath in a Scottish parliament in a nation with a long tradition of popular sovereignty might swear an oath to the people of Scotland, the people who have elected them. But that's not what happens, instead our MSPs swear an oath of allegiance to the Queen. The people don't get a look-in.

The Scotland Act which re-established the Scottish parliament specifies that new MSPs must take an oath of allegiance, although it doesn't specify the exact wording of that oath. The form of the oath is determined by the Promissory Oaths Act of 1868, which specifies the wording of the oath to be taken by public servants, elected representatives, and people who are being naturalised as British citizens. The exact wording of this oath is "I do solemnly swear to sook up to the royals, not to tsk or raise two fingers whenever Nicholas Witchell is on the telly being a sycophant, and shall refrain for now and forever from pointing out that the Windsors are a bunch of benefits claimants in fancy dress." This is usually shortened to "I do swear that I will be faithful and bear true allegiance to Her Majesty Queen Elizabeth, her heirs and successors, according to law."

A lot of MSPs have reservations about the form of the oath. An unofficial and anonymous poll of MSPs some years ago found that most would support an elected head of state to replace the monarchy. That's not really surprising for elected representatives of a nation where we celebrated the Royal Wedding with a You Know Where You Can Stick Yer Wedding party in a park in Glasgow. Republicanism is strong in Scotland, as you can tell by the collective lack of enthusiasm whenever there's some royal event or other. During the last royal nuptials, faced with a distinct lack of Scottish bunting, *Reporting Scotland* was reduced to broadcasting a piece about royal memorabilia and how much you could get if you flogged it off on eBay. The answer was, not much.

The form of the oath taken by MSPs is the same as that taken by MPs at Westminster. However the Scotland Act doesn't specify that MSPs must swear allegiance to the Queen. The Scotland Act merely states that MSPs must take an oath of allegiance; it doesn't say that MSPs can't take an oath of allegiance to the people of Scotland who elected them. Many MSPs are unhappy with the form of the oath. SNP MSPs preface it with a statement that they pledge allegiance to the people of Scotland. Labour's Neil Findlay stated that he considered the people to be citizens and not subjects.

Members of the Northern Ireland Assembly don't have to take an oath of allegiance to the Queen unless they choose to. In Stormont members swear to discharge the duties of their office in good faith, to commit to the democratic process and non-violence, and to serve all the people of Northern Ireland equally. Westminster can hardly argue that there's no precedent and that it would be unthinkable for Scotland to change the form of the oath for those of us with republican sympathies. Anyway, aren't the Unionists always arguing that Scottish politics have been Ulsterised? Changing the Scottish oath would confirm it for them. You'd think they'd be pleased. We could tell them that we're just doing it as a favour for them to give Ruth something to complain about.

There's currently a petition calling on the Scottish parliament to change the oath of allegiance to reflect more accurately the democratic sentiments of the people of Scotland. Holyrood, which we're always being told is the most devolved parliament in the history of devolving things, is surely devolved enough to be able to determine the oath that its own members must take. The Promissory Oaths Act isn't listed amongst the powers specifically reserved to Westminster, and anything not listed is devolved to Holyrood. That means that Holyrood has every right to change the wording of the oath of allegiance that new MSPs must swear.

It's about time. In a democracy the allegiance of elected representatives must be to the people who gave them a mandate. It's a change that would gain the support of most Labour MSPs and would irritate the Ruth Davidson Buffalo Fan Club no end. It would be worth doing if for no other reason than to show the Tories that they don't get to call the shots in the Scottish parliament after all and that Scotland has its own traditions and values, traditions and values which are not the same as those of the Tory Party and the British establishment.

14 May 2016

Maths star Fluffy reckons one
MP adds up to a majority

David Mundell, Scotland's very own answer to Paddington Bear, knows a lot about political mandates. Our governor general in a blue duffle coat has proclaimed from on high that the newly elected Scottish parliament with its majority of pro-independence MSPs has no mandate for a second independence referendum. Well I say proclaimed from on high, wee Fluffy was really standing on his tippy toes having a bit of a toddler strop. You need a bit more maturity to appreciate irony, otherwise the newly beardy Fluffy would appreciate the irony of a Scotland Secretary whose party managed to get a single MP elected telling a majority parliamentary force that they don't have a mandate. No mandate? Really David, you don't say. You'd think he'd have noticed seeing as how he's the single MP.

Mandates, as far as Tories are concerned, are something that applies to other people and other parties. Generally in the negative. This is because deep down inside Wee Fluffy thinks he's got a Tory superpower, the power to say that other parties don't have a mandate. Tories don't need mandates, least of all in Scotland, where you'd think by the way they're acting that they'd won the recent Holyrood elections by dint of coming a very distant second. Mind you it's easy to understand their confusion, what with them getting to govern Scotland from Westminster on the basis of having a solitary MP here. Ruthie's wee band of buffalo soldiers are taking their cue from Paddington, who's ruling Scotland with the mandate of being the only Scottish Tory who managed to get his paw into the Westminster marmalade jar.

Flush from his party's spectacular victory in the Holyrood elections, in which they boldly came a very distant second and still managed to get less of the popular vote than they did during Thatcher's time, the Scottish Secretary has been laying down the law. Fluffily Mundelly wants an end to the bickering between Holyrood and Westminster, by which he means he wants Holyrood to knuckle down and accept all the ordure thrown at it by a government that a mere fourteen per cent of Scots voted for.

Bickering, in the view of our stuffed toy representative in the UK cabinet, means pointing out that when the UK Treasury wants to use the extra powers grudgingly granted in the Scotland Bill as an excuse to lop £7 billion off the Scottish budget, this is not holding true to the principle of no detriment on which the bill is supposedly based. That's a cut that Hold 'Em to Account Ruth would have happily acquiesced to, because as far as Westminster is concerned Ruthie doesn't believe in holding to account, she believes Scotland should be a happy buffalo which is delighted that it's been castrated by its masters.

It's the job of the Scottish Secretary to make pronouncements to the people of Scotland. After all, it's not like he's actually listening to anything that any of us who are not members of Ruth's herd have to say, so there's not really much scope for dialogue. If he was listening he'd accede to the demand from the Scottish government to allow Scotland an opt-out from the Tories' hateful Trade Union Bill which is opposed by both the SNP and Labour. But Davie and his mighty mandate get to overrule everyone else in the country.

Since there is no dialogue all that leaves is him talking down to us from his seat in the cabinet, but because he's as representative of Scotland as a raised toilet seat is representative of plumbing arrangements in a convent, his pronouncements are typically as relevant to the average Scot as the future of Gaelic language broadcasting is to the honourable member for a Tory safe seat in Middle Englandshire. The difference of course is that the Tory MP has considerably more influence over the future of Gaelic broadcasting than anyone in Scotland does. Equity doesn't figure much in dealings between Scotland and the supposedly sovereign parlie on the banks of the Thames.

The only part of his pronouncement that he got right was when he said that it's not up to Nicola Sturgeon to say whether there will be a second Scottish independence referendum. Not that Nicola is currently planning a second independence referendum, because anyone who is remotely aware of Scottish politics knows that the time is not yet right for one. The right time is of course when winning it is nailed on. There's only going to be another independence referendum when a clear majority of Scots want to have one, and the chances are that they're going to vote in favour. What Fluffy hasn't quite managed to work out is that means there's only going to be another independence referendum when there is no Unionist majority in Scotland whose views must be respected.

Fluffy thinks that's a matter for Westminster to decide with its majority of Tory MPs that Scottish people didn't vote for. It's not up to Nicola Sturgeon, it's not up to David Cameron. It sure as hell isn't up to the Westminster parliament. It's up to the people of Scotland. However the Scottish Secretary isn't very keen on consulting the public after an abortive attempt to rebrand the office of the Scottish Secretary in order to better reflect the role of the voice of the UK cabinet in Scotland, only to discover that the focus group had voted overwhelmingly for the name Tory McTornface.

It may well be the legal truth that another independence referendum can only be authorised by Westminster, but legal truths must bow before political truths. The political truth is that any Westminster parliament which attempted to block a referendum which was wanted by most people in Scotland, and in which most wanted to vote Yes, would not remain the ultimate parliament for Scotland for very much longer. All it would be would be to increase support for independence. Westminster is only the ultimate parliamentary authority over Scotland because the

Scottish people, for the time being, consent to allow it to be. It's because the Westminster parliament has forgotten that political truth that the clock is ticking on the Union.

18 May 2016

We are all screwed, whatever the outcome of EU vote

Are you scared yet? Are you cowering in sheer terror? There are so many scare stories being thrown around that you should be gibbering like a maniac by now; that's exactly what commentators in the *Torygraph* are doing, although to be honest they're always like that. The only thing that's clear now from the great EU debate is that it doesn't matter which side wins in the EU referendum, we're facing the end of civilisation as we know it.

There's now less than a month to go before the vote, and both sides have already ramped up the hysteria to such an extent that their invitations to become contestants on the next series of *RuPaul's Drag Race* have been withdrawn because the programme makers don't think that level of melodrama is remotely believable. Mind you, the Leave campaign's Jacob Rees-Mogg isn't remotely believable as a human being, but that didn't stop him from being elected as a Tory MP for Somerset. Before he got involved in Conservative politics, Jakie lived in the pages of a P. G. Wodehouse novel where he had a role as a spurned fiancé.

Just a couple of months ago Cameron swore blind that he'd campaign to leave the EU if he didn't get his way with Brussels, but now he's swearing blind that it would cause an apocaplyse. Monday saw the release of a report from the Treasury which made two apocalyptic forecasts about what might happen if the UK were to leave the EU. We'll either be in the doo-doo, or we'll be in the doo doo doo doo de da da da, and the entire country not only have no job and no money, so it will just be like being back in the 1980s, we'll also have to listen to Sting go on about tantric sex. With George Osborne. Told you it would be a nightmare. Despite the fact that Treasury forecasts are typically about as reliable as Jacob Rees-Mogg's knowledge of plotlines in the Kardashians, the BBC spent the entire day reporting on Cameron and Osborne's response to a report that they themselves had published. It's a bit like interviewing a novellist and asking them for a response to their own novel, only works of fiction are usually grounded in more realism than you'll find in a UK Treasury report.

Meanwhile the Leave campaign released its new campaign video, in which we learned that if the UK leaves the EU, no one will ever get sick again and accident and emergency waiting rooms will be happy sunny places where old ladies will skip in and out in five minutes with a beam of joy on their faces, but if we stay in the EU the NHS will be overwhelmed by Turkish people seeking allergy relief because they don't have antihistamines in Ankara. The Leave campaign would have us believe that all eighty mil-lion people from Turkey and the Balkans are poised to move to Wolverhampton, but of course they vehe-mently deny that they're making immigration an issue.

Just to recap then, in case you're a sane and sensible individual and you haven't been paying attention because when you want a scary story you stream a Freddy Krueger movie from the Internet, you're going to be screwed whatever the outcome of the vote. According to the Remain campaign, if Britain votes to leave the EU your house will be worth less than one of those wee plastic houses in a Monopoly set, you won't have a job, the pound will be on a parity with the bin bag, there will be World War Three, and you'll get Boris Johnson as prime minister. Meanwhile according to the Leave campaign, if Britain votes to remain in the EU your job will be taken by a Turkish migrant, the health service will be privatised by German bureaucrats in the TTIP negotiations, there will be World War Three, and you'll get George Osborne as prime minister.

The rest of the threats from both sides might be as overblown as Donald Trump's hair, but the last ones about who gets to become prime minister are very real indeed. You're not really voting on whether the UK remains a part of the EU or leaves it, you're voting to settle the question of which ridiculous and dangerously incompetent public school buffoon gets to become the next leader of the Tory Party, and so gets to become prime minister. Should it be George Osborne with his expertise in towel folding and budgets which fold after three seconds of scrutiny, or Boris Johnson with his clown act covering for a rampant ego and a sense of entitlement that would make a Premier League footballer blush. That's your choice right there. Aren't you just thrilled that Scotland's a part of the UK? Are you scared yet? Dunno about you, but I'm terrified.

Faced with such an unappealing choice, neither side is able to make a positive case for either leaving the EU or remaining in it. It's like having to make a positive case for either staying at home to watch a three-hour documentary on the BBC about Prince Andrew's services to golf, despite knowing that the only difference between Nicholas Witchell's royalist brown-nosing and disappearing up the backside of the monarchy is depth perception and that's hard to judge on a 2D TV screen, or going to a UKIP presentation on the wit and wisdom of Nigel Farage presented by a Wee Free meenister with a bad case of haemorrhoids who had a vindaloo for his tea.

We've got a month of this left. The fact that the only people who are attempting to make a positive case are the SNP's Nicola Sturgeon, Plaid Cymru's Leanne Wood, and Caroline Lucas for the Greens tells you all you need to know about the intellectual bankruptcy of the British political system and British politicians. The only ones capable of saying anything positive are the ones who want to put an end to the British state, the only ones who are offering a choice of something other than a choice between Boris or George.

The real choice facing Scotland is whether we want our country to become an outward-looking European nation and state in its own right, making our own decisions and being in charge of our own destiny, or whether we want to remain onlookers in the Boris and George schoolyard fight. It's a no-brainer really.

25 May 2016

Bowled over by the boredom of the EU referendum

In less than three weeks the voters of Britain are to make what our political masters keep telling us is the biggest decision for a generation, if you don't count that wee votey thing we had in Scotland in 2014. Naturally Westminster doesn't count that vote as the biggest decision that voters have faced, because it was just a parochial Scottish thing and so by definition couldn't have been very important. It's a bit odd then that this supposedly most important vote in the history of voting has stirred up all the enthusiasm in Scotland that we more usually associate with indoor bowling competitions from Coatbridge. Every time you hear the announcer saying that it's about to come on the telly, a wee part of your soul shrivels up and dies while you frantically press the remote control in the hope that you can find something more interesting, like a documentary about traditional llama herders in Patagonia.

Actually that's not true, the indoor bowling doesn't come from Coatbridge any more, and there are even some people in existence who are really interested in it. Like people whose eyes light up when the presenter says the magic words that signal admittance to a mystical land of artificial lawns and where getting a jack off on the short mat isn't something that happens in an seedy nightclub for people with specialised tastes. Like the people who correct you when you make jokes about indoor bowling from Coatbridge.

There's not many of them, admittedly, but they do exist and there's a whole lot more of them than there are people who are deeply engaged with the EU referendum. No one can be bothered to correct you when you say something ridiculous about the EU referendum, which is one reason why politicians representing both the Remain and the Leave campaigns are spouting such utter utter guff.

The number of ordinary people who are passionate about the EU referendum is approximately the same as the number who think that Ruth Davidson is Scotland's most effective and interesting politician. So that would be Ruth, a handful of right-wing journalists and the guy who takes the photies for her press releases, although he's only doing it because he gets paid.

The independence referendum saw mass participation, posters in windows, local groups, local debates, the referendum was a topic that was never far from any conversation, irrespective of the way they intended to vote people were engaged, interested and passionate. Compare that to the dull sterility of the EU referendum. The media is desperately in search of a modicum of public interest, but all they're finding is an indoor bowler who's in mourning because Dougie Donnelly only seems to cover the golf these days. The indyref had wish trees, the EU ref has us wishing that they'd all go away and shut up.

The EU referendum is in fact the Ruth Davidson of referendums. It's all camera flash and no substance, all photo opportunity and no significance, all hype and no content. It's shallow and bereft of depth and each side is only interested in shouting down the other, preferably from the top of a tank. This, they claim, is holding the other side to account. Just like Ms Davidson, there's nothing meaningful or lasting, and outside a tiny self-referential circle of mutual backslappers no one cares because all it's going to decide is which careerist gets to lead the Tory Party.

In case you were wondering, the plural of referendum is referendums. Referendum is a gerund in Latin, an impersonal and abstract part of the verbal system and as such has no plural. Referendum only requires a plural because it was borrowed into English as a noun, and therefore only requires a plural due to the demands of English grammar, not Latin grammar. So the only appropriate plural is the English one, referendums, not the pseudo-Latin referenda. Even Boris Johnson gets that wrong and he's supposedly an expert in the classics, so all I can say is Playing Fields of Eton Nil, Coatbridge Comprehensive 1. This wee detour into grammar is more interesting to most people than the EU referendum in Scotland; that's how little engagement there is with the topic which is dominant in the minds of the big girls and boys of Westminster.

The failure of the EU referendum to engage and excite the public in Scotland is a sign of just how estranged most of the country has become from the politics of Westminster. Both sides compete to scare voters the most, resulting in a stalemate which isn't matey but which is very stale indeed.

This isn't our referendum, it's a vote in which Scotland's voice will be swamped by louder and more shouty voices from elsewhere, and where any decision we make will be unlikely to affect the final outcome. The only interest Scotland has is what will happen if the rest of the UK votes to leave but Scotland votes to remain. Then things could get very interesting indeed.

4 June 2016

Logic puts Brexiteers like Boris Johnson in the pro-indy camp

Tomorrow Nicola Sturgeon is going to do what Davie Cameron refuses to do: have a debate with Boris Johnson, one of the leading figures in the campaign to get the UK to vote to leave the EU. Davie refused to debate with Alex Salmond during the Scottish independence referendum campaign, claiming that the vote was a matter for Scots alone, although this didn't stop him sticking his oar in at every available opportunity. The real reason was of course fear that he'd have his backside handed to him on a plate like roasted bacon.

Boris Johnson has an approach to politics like the Roman historian Tacitus doing comedic pratfalls, whoops there goes my toga. It's Roman gladiators with custard pies as a distraction to make us all giggle while the powerful throw the poor to the lions, and Davie's brand of oleaginous PR schmooze just can't compete in the attention-getting stakes. This time his excuse for refusing a debate is that Davie debating another top Tory would only make the media focus on Tory disputes, and not on the EU issues at hand. He doesn't want anyone to intrude on the Conservative Party's private grief as it rips out its own intestines despite the fact that this is easily the most entertaining part of the EU debate for most of us.

In other words, for Davie the interests of the party trump the interests of the country, a tale that's been told of both the Conservatives and Labour over many decades. But then the only reason that this referendum is being held is to settle the internal Tory dispute over Europe and as a proxy party leadership contest. It was always party before country, and always will be. It's how the Westminster system works.

Because Davie won't debate his old school chum Boris, Nicola Sturgeon is going to have to do the job instead. Already the apologists for demonising the poor, beating up the unemployed and kicking away the crutches of disabled people, otherwise known as the right-wing press, have been wondering aloud how it can be that the SNP supports one Union, the European one, yet is so firmly against another Union, the British one. You can be certain that Boris is going to bring that point up, quite possibly in connection with an obscure classical reference. But then the man who once claimed that a pound of government money spent in Croydon was more valuable and useful than a pound spent in Scotland really ought to have worked out for himself why it is that so many of us north of the border are less than enamoured with right-wing British nationalist politicians like Boris.

We could just as easily ask why it is that politicians like Boris or Michael Gove who stride the stage pronouncing that they think it's unfair that a country has laws imposed on it by people that it didn't vote for don't also support Scottish independence. Funnily enough the right-wing commentators who ask rhetorically why the Scottish government supports the

EU but wants independence for Scotland never stop to ask themselves that question. The answer to that inconsistency is of course British nationalism. They don't think that Scotland is really a country, just a region that should trot along while important national politicians like Boris decide where to spend a pound of our tax money.

Claiming that it's inconsistent to support Scottish independence while remaining a part of the EU is a bit like claiming that it's intellectually and morally inconsistent for a person to like marmalade but hate Marmite, even though both can be spread on toasted baked goods and start with the letter M. Although in the case of the British union it might be more accurate to describe it as a bitter, rancid and unhealthy paste which clogs Scotland's arteries, leaves a sour taste in the mouth and has long since passed its use-by date.

The EU doesn't set our budget and tell us how much we've got to spend on public services. It doesn't determine our retirement age or pensions, our benefits or social security. The EU doesn't collect our taxes and give us back what it tells us we're entitled to. The EU doesn't impose nuclear weapons on us and site them just outside our largest city. The EU doesn't tell us that we're going to invade some Middle Eastern country that many of us would struggle to locate on a map. The EU doesn't control our broadcasting and refuse to allow us a national public service broadcaster of our own. The EU doesn't make our representatives second class in its parliament even though the UK has opt-outs on many areas of European legislation. Westminster does all these things despite the fact that Scotland is represented in the UK government by a single solitary Tory MP. Likening the control over the UK that the EU has to Westminster's control over Scotland is like comparing attendance at a nightclub with having your neck held tight in a stranglehold while the breath is choked out of you.

But the biggest difference of all is that the EU is a union of sovereign states which have agreed to pool sovereignty in certain restricted areas for the common good of the union as a whole. The United Kingdom is an incorporating union in which all sovereignty rests with the Westminster parliament. The member states of the EU are recognised as sovereign entities by all other EU members, the member countries of the UK are not recognised as sovereign entities by the UK parliament or politicians like Boris. The other members of the EU cannot force the UK to remain a member of the EU against its will, but British politicians like Boris or Ruth Davidson believe that the rest of the UK should be able to force Scotland out of the EU against its will. It's even easier to put party before country when you affect not to believe that the country exists.

On Thursday evening, Nicola Sturgeon will remind Boris Johnson that Scotland will make up its own mind about its membership of both the EU and the UK. If Boris wants Scotland to remain a member of the UK he's going to have to show this country considerably more respect than he has done so far.

8 June 2016

Tories will suffer for broken EU promises

George Osborne was in Scotland this week, visiting a farm in the Borders with Ruth Davidson in the latest episode of the Remain campaign's Project Fear. George and Ruth visited some sheep on the farm, carefully avoiding the pigs because Davie Cameron has got first dibs on them, but sheep are the Tories' natural constituency anyway. They're the ones who're always saying SNPbaaaad.

George and Ruth were sheep whispering in an effort to tell people in Scotland that the SNP doesn't have a mandate for another independence referendum while simultaneously telling people in the rest of the UK that they need to vote Remain in order to ensure that the SNP can't have one under any circumstance. The SNP didn't win the last election, oh no, said Ruthie, labouring under the delusion that she'd won it by dint of coming a very distant second. They didn't get a mandate for having another independence referendum, so they're just going to have to jolly well put up and shut up, so there, or I'll just have to get even more ranty than normal at Furst Meenister's Questions.

Tories are forever making authoritative statements about things they know to be untrue, as Nicola Sturgeon pointed out to Boris Johnson during the

EU debate on Thursday. This is because for Tories, poshness is a substitute for accuracy and facts. Ruth isn't very posh, just shouty, and despite her contrafactual assertions, the SNP may well have considerably more of a mandate for holding a second independence referendum in the event of a Brexit than the Tories do for holding the EU referendum in the first place. Allegations continue to pile up that the Conservatives only won the general election by committing electoral expenses fraud. Over two dozen Tory MPs are now having their election victories investigated by the authorities, and if the allegations are held up the Conservatives will have no majority in the Commons at all, and plunging the country into this current EU referendum will have been done illegitimately.

Ruth Davidson and George Osborne act as though denial is a tributary of declyde, but there is actually a majority of pro-independence MSPs in the current Scottish parliament. Ruth might affect to believe that the SNP lost its majority so can't pass a referendum bill, but there are more SNP MSPs than MSPs from all three Unionist parties combined, and when the Greens are taken into account there is an absolute majority for independence. There is not a shred of doubt that the pro-independence parties won their majority entirely honestly and fairly. That is something which cannot be said for the Conservatives in Westminster.

The people of Scotland voted for that pro-independence majority in the full knowledge that the Conservatives were going to hold their EU referendum, just like when we voted to remain a part of the UK back in September 2014 we did so on the basis that Westminster swore blind that doing so was the only way to ensure that Scotland remained a part of the EU.

There's a very real possiblity that a majority of people in the UK will vote for a Brexit, and if that happens it will have come about because large numbers of people feel disenfranchised and alienated by our political establishment. One of the major causes of that disenchantment is that politicians like George Osborne and Ruth Davidson can make promises and commitments like promising that only with a No vote would Scotland be secure within the EU, and then renege on their promises a few months later. Their current panic over the possibility of a Brexit is a strategic error entirely of their own making, and they're bent on repeating that error with the prospect of another Scottish referendum.

Anyone with a modicum of expertise in the finer points of contract law, which is anyone who has ever watched an episode of *Judge Judy*, knows that when a promise or commitment is made and a deal struck on that basis, one party to the deal can't later change the terms of the deal and expect the other party to hold to their end of it. Judge Judy gets very stern about that sort of thing. She makes a face and rips the guilty party apart like a ferocious wee dug disguised as an elderly American lady. Ruthie and George would get short shrift from Judy. They'd be the feckless boyfriend trying to explain that when Scotland loaned the UK its vote in September 2014 in return for EU membership that it was in fact a gift for the UK to squander on a new tank for Ruth and they didn't have to bother their wee heids about the promise that in return for our votes we could stay in the EU.

The Westminster parliament and the Better Together campaign of which the Conservatives were a part made a deal with the Scottish electorate when they inveigled us into a No vote in no small measure on the basis of Scotland's status in the EU. They have no right to go back on that deal now, and if they do then there is a natural consequence. That consequence is that the gemme of the first independence referendum is a bogey. There will be a rematch. And there won't be a thing that Ruth can do to stop it.

11 June 2016

If your god says hate, maybe it's your demons talking

It's said that people pay closest attention to those parts of their holy books that happen to confirm their existing prejudices. The parts that they read most assiduously are those parts that allow them to say that their god instructs them to hate people whom they already hate, while ignoring the parts that say that their god wants them to love, to demonstrate compassion, to understand, to accept.

That's particularly the case with those like the perpetrator of the Orlando atrocity who carried out the most lethal homophobic hate crime against LGBT people since the Nazi persecution during WW2. Omar Mateen might have chosen to seek justification for his hatred in his particular holy book, but that's not where he learned how to hate gay people. He just paid most attention to those parts of it that happened to confirm prejudices that he already had. His holy book is where he happened to find a spurious cover for his own shortcomings, his own inadequacies, his own fear and his own insecurity in his masculinity. He could just as easily have found it in the Bible, or in any other sacred text, or in just about any political ideology.

David Copeland, the neo-Nazi nail bomber who blew up a gay bar in London's Soho in 1999, killing three and maiming dozens more, sought justification for his hatred of gay people in a perverse far right ideology. He hated Muslims as much as he hated LGBT people, but his hatred of gay people probably stemmed from similar motivations to those of Omar Mateen, a deep-rooted insecurity in his own masculinity which he tried to compensate for by demonising other groups. According to some reports Copeland was influenced in his violent beliefs by a pamphlet written by a certain David Myatt, another white supremacist and homophobe. Myatt later converted to radical Islamic extremism and defended the killing of civilians and praised Osama bin Laden. He has now reportedly renounced violence and extremism.

The victims of Omar Mateen probably included heterosexual people as well as LGBT people. Amongst the victims of David Copeland was a straight pregant woman who was out celebrating with her husband and their gay friends. Mateen and Copeland attacked tolerance and inclusion as much as they attacked a sexual minority. They attacked the acceptance of LGBT people by their straight families and friends.

Nevertheless the motive for the attack was the hatred of LGBT people. It was shameful that sections of the media attempted to overlook this aspect of the crime. The *Daily Mail* initially ignored the attack entirely on its front page, to make room for its special offer of pearl earrings just like the Queen's instead. Left-wing commentator Owen Jones stormed out of a press review on *Sky News* to applause in this household as the presenter attempted to downplay Mateen's motivation in hateful homophobia and talk about Islamic extremism instead. As Jones pointed out, if Mateen had chosen to attack a synagogue instead, no one would have denied or downplayed the fact that the atrocity was anti-Semitic.

Mateen was born and brought up in the USA, a country where the Christian right has a long history of stoking the fires of homophobia in order to score political points. Even while those wounded in the Orlando attack were receiving first aid in the emergency rooms of Florida hospitals Dan Patrick, the Republican Lt. Governor of Texas, tweeted that the LGBT victims had reaped what they had sown as a punishment for mocking God. Just as we cannot separate the crime from the ease with with anyone with a grudge can access firearms in the USA, we cannot separate it from the climate of hatred fostered by certain right-wing American politicians of a decidedly non-Islamic bent.

Perhaps the day will come when people will realise that if they believe that their god teaches them to hate gay people, to kill peaceful shopkeepers because of supposed heresy, to exclude and diminish women, that they're not worshipping a god at all. They're worshipping the demons that live within themselves.

For generations LGBT people have faced violence, exclusion, intolerance. We were afraid, and often still are afraid, to walk down the street holding the hand of our loved one, afraid to casually mention in conversation that we have a significant other of the same gender as ourselves. But gradually, we've come out into the open, we've learned to live and love as equals of heterosexual people, and by and large we have found the acceptance of heterosexual people.

Scotland has done particularly well in this regard. I'd be the last person to deny that there are still challenges, that I'd still be wary about walking down Shettleston Road hand in hand with my significant other. Young LGBT people in Scotland still face exclusion, intolerance and a lack of acceptance. But we have travelled across the galaxy compared to when I was a young gay man in a working-class community in the East End of Glasgow in the late 1970s, facing universal condemnation, afraid that if anyone discovered my secret that I'd be cast out, beaten up and abused, all the while listening to a daily litany of homophobic hate speech that passed for banter. It was just a joke, don't take it seriously. Now LGBT Scots find ourselves in the incredible situation where abusing us because of our sexual orientation or gender identity counts as a hate crime, but instead the UK media abuses the us all, gay or straight, because we're Scottish. Anti-Scottish racism, it's the new homophobic banter.

In the days after the attack there were spontaneous demonstrations of solidarity and support in London's Soho and in Glasgow's George Square. All across the world people gay and straight stood up and held hands and said no to violence, no to intolerance, no to fear. Mateen will not succeed in driving us back into the darkness of the closet any more than

Copeland did. We are the ones who walk in love. We are the ones who walk in the light. We are the ones who practise what a real god preaches – love, peace, compassion and mercy. That's why we are winning, that's why we are going to win.

15 June 2016

Best EU referendum outcome is lose-lose for Tories

This EU referendum campaign is like getting a tooth extraction without anaesthetic from an unsympathetic dentist. It alternates periods of pain with squirming squeamishness and all you can do is stare at the clock as you count down the minutes until it's all over. And you know that however the procedure turns out it's going to cost you and will leave lasting wounds that will take forever to heal. The clock is now counting down the final minutes, and soon it will all be over. Or at least this part of it.

I started off this campaign as an enthusiastic supporter of Remain. I lived in Europe for many years. The dug is an EU canine migrant into Scotland and entered this country on a Spanish EU pet passport. I'm fluent in Spanish and genuinely believed in the European project. I naively hoped that someone in the official Remain campaign would try and make a positive case for a European project that was founded with the most noble of ideals, as an attempt to put the spectre of war behind Europe forever and to build a united continent where we are all more conscious of what we share than we are of what divides us. And by and large, despite its many faults and failures, the European project has succeeded in that.

However, the campaign to remain in the EU has been so godawful that I've come to believe that they really do not deserve to win. Winning would only put a smug smile on the shiny face of a David Cameron who has conducted the entire proceedings as a campaign to save his sorry career. I don't want to give him the satisfaction. The official Remain campaign has been like a campaign for vegetarianism that's only succeeded in persuading lifelong vegans to rush out to buy the latest Hannibal Lecter cookbook, *Serving Suggestions for Conservative MPs*. It's shorter than his previous works as Tory MPs have no heart, brains or backbone, just plenty of gall and that's inedible.

I think to myself that if the Remain campaign has been so hapless, half-baked and hopeless as to alienate someone like me who started off with rock-solid European credentials, just what has it done to people who were unsure about it to begin with. The Remain campaign has been even worse than the Better Together campaign in its relentless negativity, its scaremongering and its utter lack of any positive vision for remaining in Europe. There's only one campaign that I can think of that's even more lamentable, and that's the campaign to leave the EU.

The Leave campaign has matched the Remain campaign scare for scare, fearmongering for fearmongering, and has added a nasty dose of racism that has inflamed the British body politic like a strep infection. Much as it sticks in my throat like a Tory gall pie to see the Remain campaign win and Davie Cameron act like a victor, the victory of the Leave campaign would give that role to Boris Johnson, and that would be worse. Not much worse, it has to be said: one smug Tory with a rampant sense of entitlement is much the same as another smug Tory with a rampant sense of entitlement. But it would still be worse, because it would strip us of our status as European citizens and put at risk our connections with the rest of the continent.

One of the Remain campaign's many scare stories this week was that a Brexit would make the UK the most hated country in Europe, but in truth it is already as popular as George Osborne's liver pâté at a vegetarian buffet. That's why we keep getting null points in *Eurovision*. No one likes the UK enough to form a voting bloc with us, not even Ireland. The UK is already treading on thin ice as far as the tolerance and patience of other European nations is concerned. A Brexit wouldn't just make the UK fall through the ice, the Tories would be taking a blowtorch to it in the hopes that they could sail off into the mid-Atlantic to seek a mythical special relationship with the USA.

Tomorrow I'll be voting purely in Scotland's interests. I'm going to vote in the way which has the best chance of producing a second independence referendum and wiping the smug grins off both sets of entitled Tories. I'm voting to remain, not because I'm sold on the Remain campaign's scare stories, threats and menaces, but because only a Remain vote in Scotland combined with a Leave vote in the rest of the UK will produce the justification for a second independence referendum. There are no guarantees that will happen of course, but in the event it doesn't I'd rather suffer smug Tories while retaining my rights as a European citizen than suffering smug Tories without them.

In an ideal world, maybe somewhere in that infinity of parallel universes that some theories in physics tell us must exist, it is possible for both campaigns to lose simultaneously. If there's an infinite number of universes then logically that must be possible. Although that said there still isn't any universe anywhere in which Nigel Farage isn't less irritating than a urinary tract infection. Both campaigns losing is certainly what they deserve, but sadly it's not going to happen in this universe.

So I'm just going to hold out for my ideal result instead. It's highly unlikely to come to pass, but what I really want now is for the rest of the UK to vote narrowly to leave, but Scotland to vote strongly to remain, and then the UK as a whole will have to remain a member of the EU because Scotland said so. That will really wipe the smug grins off all the Tories. The Brexiteers will have lost, and the Cameroons will have lost England. That's the closest we can get to both sides losing. If you live in Scotland vote Remain, and with a bit of luck we can make both Boris and Davie cry.

22 June 2016

This result must be our cue to break free and become independent

The independence referendum was won for the No campaign on a fantasy, a fictional UK that existed purely in the imaginations of the Unionist parties. Vote No, they said, for jobs that would be safe, vote No for shipbuilders. Only the jobs were never safe and the ships would never sail. Vote No, they said, for pensions that would be secure. Only the pensions have never been more insecure as the markets tank and the pound plummets. Vote No, they said, for greater powers and the most devolved parliament possible. Only that turned out to be some tinkering with taxes and powers over road signs, and English votes for English laws. It meant road signs that said "No entry". Vote No, they said, for a Scotland that was shielded and sheltered within the EU. Only now we're being ripped out of the EU against our express will and left unshielded and unsheltered in the blistering cold winds of the demagoguery of Boris and Nigel.

When you enter a contract on the basis of a lie, the contract is void. The Unionist parties' contract with Scotland has been voided by the actions of the Westminster parliament. It wasn't Scotland which broke the Union. It was the Unionist parties which broke two unions. This is the biggest betrayal of their contract of trust with the people of Scotland, even bigger than English votes for English laws, even bigger than their neutering of the Smith Commission. Scotland is to be taken out of the EU even though we've voted to remain members by a considerably larger margin than we voted to remain a part of the UK. When you have irreconcilible differences, something has to give. And it won't be Scotland this time.

When you don't deliver what you promised in order to secure a vote, you lose any right to demand that the result of the vote is respected. When the best of both worlds means being bested by Boris, there's no place left for Scotland within the UK. It's not just the SNP that needs to be held to account. It's the Unionist parties too. They promised Scotland something which they could not deliver. They promised the broad shoulders and the embrace of the UK. Only that embrace is crushing the life out of us.

Scotland spoke on Thursday, and Scotland said it was a proud European nation. That vote must be respected too. It would be a travesty of democracy for the Unionist parties to insist that Scotland must be torn out of Europe, even though every single council area in the country returned a majority vote for Remain, while hypocritically demanding respect for a vote two years ago that they won on a false prospectus.

So now we stand before another independence referendum, another chance to decide whether Scotland should be a respected and equal member of a union of European nations, or a passenger at the back of the Boris bus, driving off to a destination to which we've said we don't want to go. We should weep for our English and Welsh friends who are left to brave the gales of the Tory right as they take their country off into a mid-Atlantic Thatcherite dystopia, but the best way to help them is to create an example of something better. We can build a Scotland founded on equality and tolerance, on inclusion and diversity. Or we can meekly submerge ourselves in a UK in which Nigel Farage is a national hero, where Scotland's opinions count for as much as a euro coin in a UKIP bar.

Scotland staying in the UK out of a misplaced sense of solidarity with our English and Welsh sisters and brothers will do nothing to help them, and will only destroy us. There is a difference between solidarity and a suicide pact. True solidarity means the creation of hope. Let's create hope, for the people of Scotland, for the poor and the marginalised, for the low-paid and the excluded. Let's grasp this second chance, let's not waste it.

We have work to do. The Scottish government must reach out to the EU, to gain assurances that Scotland can inherit the membership of the UK, with its opt-outs on Schengen and the euro. We need a plan for a Scottish currency. We need to assuage the doubts that went unanswered last time. But we start from a much stronger position than before. There is no phalanx of Scottish Unionist MPs in Westminster. The Labour Party has been brought down and humbled and won't be so dogmatically opposed to independence as before. The idea of independence has been politically normalised and brought right into the mainstream of Scottish politics where before it was on the margins.

But above all, we have a people who have experience of mobilising themselves, of creating a grassroots campaign. We know how to get our message out. We are not working as though we were in the early days of a better nation. We are working because we already are in those days. We are working to make a better Scotland a reality.

25 June 2016

It's time to escape the ugly new Britain

Remember during the independence referendum, when all these big beasts from Westminster kept telling silly wee Scotland that we needed the broad shoulders of the United Kingdom? Well here we are, in the middle of the biggest self-inflicted crisis since Baron Frankenstein decided to make a monster, with the predictable result that angry townspeople are getting out the torches and pitchforks, and what do we discover? Those broad shoulders of the United Kingdom don't have a head on them. Chickens can keep running about after decapitation because they've got a bundle of nerve cells in their spinal columns, which means that a headless chicken has got more of a functioning neural system than the government of the United Kingdom.

No one in the Conservative Party has the slightest idea about what to do next now that their jolly jape of a referendum as a proxy for a leadership contest has taken the UK out of the EU, broken the United Kingdom, put a bomb under the Irish peace process, set off an ugly spate of racist incidents throughout England, and caused a chasm in public opinion deeper and wider than the Grand Canyon. The Leave campaign is denying all the claims that it was making just a few days ago. £350 million? Oh no, we never said we'd invest it in the NHS. Stirring up racism? How very dare you suggest we did any such thing? Losing the UK's AAA credit rating? Eh, that wasn't supposed to happen.

The Tories are only sure of two things now, firstly that a Remain vote would have made Scottish independence far more difficult, and that now there's a Leave vote that's also made Scottish independence far more difficult. Secondly they are quite certain that Scotland shouldn't have another independence referendum, because that would be divisive. Well they know a lot about creating divisiveness don't they, although apparently not so much about irony, and there was us thinking that irony was supposed to be a British value.

But don't panic, Number 10 has announced that Oliver Letwin is in charge of Brexit preparations for the time being. Letwin's career is littered with more embarrassing gaffes than Prince Philip's. That's the Oliver Letwin that left a pile of sensitive government papers in a bin in a park. All the EU needs to do to discover the UK's negotiating position is keep an eye on rubbish collections in the Whitehall area.

The Conservatives are more interested in their leadership contest than they are in the fate of the country. They're happy to hold an entire continent hostage to the decisions of the parliamentary Conservative Party and Boris Johnson's career. On *Sky News* over the weekend political editor Faisal Islam reported that Boris's Leave campaign have no plan at all about what to do over the coming months. They don't know what sort of Brexit they want, they don't know how to go about getting it once they do decide, and they seem to think that they'll be able to prevent the free movement of European Union citizens into the UK while preserving the right of British citizens to live and work in Europe. That's the Tory legacy, the result of their implacable belief that the UK is a special little snowflake to which normal rules don't apply. The Conservatives have created a bigger political vacuum than the empty space between Boris's ears.

There is no government, there is no official Opposition either. We don't have a Labour shadow cabinet any more. All that's left is a broken breakfast tray bearing nothing but the stale toast of Jeremy Corbyn's leadership. Members of the shadow cabinet have been dropping off more quickly than attendees at the Scottish Tory Party conference. Corbyn is refusing to resign, although he's now leading a party that is refusing to be led by him. The Blairites are in open revolt, although to be honest they were pretty revolting to begin with.

The Blairites haven't mounted their attempt to oust Corbyn just now because they're afraid he can't win an election. With a shattered Conservative Party in meltdown, the Blairites are afraid that he can. That they're using a time of national crisis to mount a leadership coup tells you all you need to know about their concern for the national interest. One after another they make a sad-eyed press statement announcing their resignation, saying, "I deeply regret standing down from the shadow cabinet and am coordinating my resignation with my colleagues in order to inflict the maximum possible damage."

Their sudden haste to blame Corbyn for the Brexit may or may not be related to the impending publication of the Chilcot report after a delay of many years. Although it's quite likely that the report will be delayed even longer as Chilcot seems to be the guy who's going to be put in charge of Brexit negotiations.

Labour has no shadow Scottish Secretary now, following the resignation of Ian Murray. Since the pool of Scottish MPs consists of Ian Murray in a bathtub with a Union Jack rubber duck, Corbyn's going to have a hard time replacing him. The truth is, they probably don't need to bother. Scotland has no need for the parliamentary Labour Party, just as we have no need for the Tories.

Both the main parties in the United Kingdom are as rudderless and adrift as Ian's Union Jack rubber duck. That the only functioning government in the United Kingdom right now is the one that wants to remain in the EU and leave the UK tells you all you need to know about the depth of the pile of doggy doo that Britain is in. It reaches all they down into the black heart of Hell, or of Nigel Farage, which is much the same thing. Britain has become an ugly and inward-looking place. Scotland needs to escape.

Events are happening so quickly that it's difficult to keep up. Between the time this article is written and it is published, Scotland could very well be independent already. All over the land former No voters have looked upon the mess that the United Kingdom has turned into, and decided that we're really not better together with dysfunction after all. And to their credit, most Yes voters have been remarkably restrained with the I-told-you-soes. We are welcoming them into the fold; all of us want what's best for Scotland, all of us want a Scotland that's international, outward-looking, and accepting of migrants and our European friends and allies.

Irrespective of our political affiliations we all agree with Angus Robertson's statement in the House of Commons on Monday: "We have no intention whatsoever of seeing Scotland taken out of the EU." We're going to keep the dream of that European, social democratic, tolerant Scotland alive during these difficult days, and we're going to make it a reality. Yesterday in the European Parliament the SNP MEP Alyn Smith made an impassioned plea for Scotland to remain in the EU, and received a standing ovation. Scotland has allies. We are not alone.

We're in a whole new world now. The days when England ordered and Scotland meekly followed are over. Westminster better get used to it.

29 June 2016

Unionists are going nuclear on us already

The starting pistol hasn't even been fired on a second independence referendum and already Project Fear Mark III has been lobbing the usual scarebombs into the debate. We've already had the traditional Spanish Veto threat, even though it's as likely that Mariano Rajoy will veto an independent Scotland's membership of the EU as he would dance up and down the Royal Mile naked singing that Gibraltar is British.

Rajoy's bluff is played up to the max by politicans whose knowledge of Spanish politics is as poor as that of those whom they hope to convince with the bluff. The truth of the matter is that the second there's a Yes vote in a second independence referendum, the Spanish government will immediately declare that it had been saying all along that the Scottish situation was nothing at all like that of Catalonia. Then Mariano Rajoy will be able to sleep secure at night knowing that his local party won't be unceremoniously dumped by the Galician fishing interests who are its biggest funders. That would leave his party coffers as empty as the fish counter in a Spanish supermarket would be if he'd vetoed Scottish membership and along with it vetoed Spain's access to Scottish fishing grounds.

Hot on the heels of the predictable Iberian red rag of Unionist bull came the non-news from a Thatcherite think tank that Scotland would be just like Greece only without the sunshine. This comes under the heading of "Well they would say that wouldn't they?" I've never been entirely sure why Unionists think that it benefits them to harp on about how poor Scotland is. For the past 300 years the levers of economic control in Scotland have been firmly in the hands of the Westminster parliament.

Scotland is in a geopolitically stable part of the globe. We are blessed with an embarrassment of natural resources, including being in the enviable position of being more than self-sufficient in energy. In fact we've got energy resources coming out of our fracking ears. We've got a highly educated English-speaking population. We've got four universities in the world's top one hundred. We've got a long record of innovation and invention. And unlike Greece we've got a tax collection agency that actually functions. If you wanted a recipe for a prosperous independent nation, you'd start off with Scotland's ingredients. Yet according to Maggie Thatcher's favourite think tank Scotland is a basket case that would be poorer than Greece.

For a think tank their thinking is pretty narrow and limited. If that's the conclusion that you come to after examining the Scottish economy, anyone who was capable of joined-up thinking would immediately think to ask whose fault it was that Scotland was so badly off that it was incapable of looking after itself. And the answer could only be that the fault lies fairly and squarely with the Westminster Unionist parliament which has been misruling and mismanaging Scotland for these past 300 years. This is not an advertisement for continuing Westminster rule.

The Unionist parties don't want us to think to ask these questions, and the Unionist media certainly isn't going to ask them either. Indyref1 was characterised by forensic investigation of all the claims of the Yes campaign, while Better Together got a free pass. Indyref2 is shaping up to be the same. So let's get some retaliation in early. With Theresa May, the favourite for the Tory leadership, saying she wants to press ahead with the renewal of Trident, the issue of nuclear weaponry is going to loom large in the next independence referendum just as it did in the last one.

I want an independent Scotland that's nuclear free and neutral, outside NATO, but an argument frequently aired during the last independence referendum campaign was that Scotland wouldn't be allowed to get rid of the nukes from the Clyde and then go on to join NATO. Personally I don't want Scotland to be in NATO, but I also want the next independence referendum to be characterised by accurate information. We won't get that from the Unionist press.

The argument that Scotland would not be able to get rid of the nukes from Faslane then go on to join NATO was made repeatedly by a number of Unionist figures, and not once was it challenged by a mainstream media which clearly refused to do the most basic of research. The situation of a country getting rid of nuclear subs and missiles from its territory and then going on to join NATO is not unprecedented. Another country has done exactly that before, not that our Unionist media ever bothered to tell anyone about it.

In the post-WW2 era Spain was friendless as although the dictator Franco had kept his ruined country neutral as it recovered from the civil war, he made the mistake of cosying up to Hitler and Mussolini. In an effort to sook up to the USA, Franco allowed the Americans to build a nuclear submarine base at Rota, close to the city of Cadiz in southern Spain. This was massively unpopular with the Spanish people, especially after a US plane laden with nuclear warheads crashed into the sea as it approached the base, narrowly avoiding a major nuclear disaster.

After Franco died late in 1975, Spain began to transition to democracy. One of the priorities for the new democratic government was to rid the country of the American missile base. Negotiations began with the USA on removing the nuclear weapons. The negotiations were concluded and a treaty signed. The missiles and subs were gone from Spain before the end of the decade. Spain became a member of NATO in 1982 after its transition to democracy was deemed to be complete.

All this information is in the public domain. None of it is secret. Yet the British Unionist media did not report on any of it when Unionist politicians were claiming that it was going to be impossible for Scotland to rid itself of the nuclear obscenity on the Clyde. As I said above, I am no fan of NATO membership for an independent Scotland, but as our country stands on the brink of a second independence referendum, it is important that the people of Scotland know that it is perfectly possible for a country to rid itself of nuclear weaponry and still maintain good relationships with other countries in Europe and North America. Spain got rid of another country's nuclear missiles and then went on to join NATO.

Scotland, if it wanted to, could do exactly the same. The moral to take from this story is that it will be perfectly possible for an independent Scotland to rid itself of nuclear weapons within a couple of years, and it will be able to do so without prejudicing its relationships with NATO countries, whether we choose to join NATO or not. Independence gives us that choice, remaining in the UK doesn't.

6 July 2016

May's not the only one who can be difficult

All we ever get these days is bad news from Westminster. It makes you nostalgic for the days when the worst thing on a news report was that there was horsemeat in supermarket lasagne. UK politics went from bad to worse some time back, and is now plunging its way through the frozen floor of the lowest level of Hell, the one that Dante said was reserved for telemarketers and Simon Cowell. Theresa May is the new prime minister of UK.

By virtue of being the prime minister of the UK, Theresa May is therefore also the prime minister of Scotland, despite the fact that Fluffy Mundell was the only person in the entire country who voted for her. She was hailed by the Conservative Party as the country's best hope, but that's only if you're hoping for authoritarian xenophobic reactionary right-wing austerity on steroids. That's the Theresa May who said last year that the prospect of the SNP having any influence on the UK government would provoke the biggest crisis since the abdication.

Now Britain is in the middle of the biggest crisis since the abdication, caused entirely by Ms May's Tory colleagues, and she's only becoming PM because the ones responsible for the crisis have abdicated. None of the prominent Brexiteers are left standing. Except

Liam Fox, who is still hoping that he'll get a place in Theresa May's cabinet as Minister of State for Adam Werritty. As the country came to the realisation that Theresa May was going to become prime minister, she said that she wanted to build a country that works for everyone, although she didn't explain why she's spent her entire time in Westminster voting for legislation that does the exact opposite. Possibly, and I am not making this up, it's because she's got a cat.

This prime minister with the support of no one in the country who isn't actually a stuffed toy is going to take Scotland out of the EU even though Scots voted by a very large majority to retain our EU membership, and despite the fact that we were told by Ms May's chums not two years ago that the only way we could ensure our EU membership was by voting to remain a part of the UK. That's how democracy works in the UK. You get more of a choice in voting for *Big Brother* contestants than you do for the prime minister or whether Scotland is a part of the EU or not.

Not-Mother Theresa's coronation as PM came after her opponent Mother Andrea Leadsom decided that maybe she'd be better off honing her parenting skills with under-fives as it turned out that Tory MPs were too immature for her after all. Instead of a Conservative Party election, we're getting a Conservative coronation instead, only without any bunting or street parties. Mind you, it's also a coronation where we don't have to suffer Nicholas Witchell's wittering royalist sycophancy, so it's not all bad. We just have the wittering sycophancy of the Tory press instead.

Brexit means Brexit, said Theresa in her first address to the press. She's not disposed to compromise on the freedom of movement, and she boasted that the EU is going to discover that she's a difficult woman. She can be as difficult as she likes, but the truth of the matter is that the UK has a very weak position. Difficult or not, she's not going to dictate the terms of the Brexit. That will be the EU that's doing that.

Our new kitten-heeled ruler has promised to deliver a Better Britain, but it won't be a better Britain for the poor, and it certainly won't be better for the working-class voters who were seduced by the Brexit message. Free from the constraints imposed by the EU and the European Human Rights legislation, Britain is going to be a cold, unwelcoming and hard place. The only freedoms will be the freedom of business to exploit, the freedom to privatise, and the freedom of the state to snoop and spy. And it will all be dressed up in red, white and blue bunting with patriotic parades and cooing at royal babies.

Somewhere on her very long list of problems to address, May is going to have to address her Scottish problem. All Tory prime ministers have a Scottish problem, on account of the fact that over large tracts of the country the word Tory is understood as a term of abuse, however Theresa May has a very particular Scottish problem. This is because not only is Tory still a term of abuse over much of the country, but the country has just voted to remain a part of the EU by a very considerable margin, a margin far larger than the margin by which it voted to remain a part of the UK two years ago. Now all the promises made by the Better Together campaign lie in the dust along with the Brexiteers' career prospects, and opinion polls show that there's no longer a 55 per cent pro-Union majority whose wishes must be respected.

Worse than that, at least for Theresa, is that Scotland has a government which was elected with a clear mandate to hold another independence referendum if there was a material change in circumstances. Theresa can stamp down her kitten heel leopard print shoes all she likes, but there's not much she can do to stop Scotland sailing off into the European distance. It's not just Theresa who can be a difficult woman. The Scottish government can withhold legislative consent to those parts of Brexit that are devolved responsibilities. We could be difficult in other ways too. The EU might not look too kindly on a Westminster which was seeking Brexit compromises while it attempted to block Scotland's attempts to remain a part of the EU. In any event, Westminster refusing to allow a referendum is the guaranteed way of ensuring that Scotland will vote for independence. Theresa May is going to discover that Scotland is full of difficult women and men.

13 July 2016

Sense of déjà vu as a new batch of tories prepare to lord it over Scotland

Are you ready to bow down before your new Tory overlords, Scotland? Although to be honest the new Tory overlords look suspiciously like the last Tory overlords. Same overweening sense of entitlement, same telling Scotland what we can or cannot do on the basis of having a single MP here, same complaining that the EU is undemocratic because we don't vote for it, same irony bypass. The new Mayday government is being touted as blue-collar Conservatism because it's no longer headed by a bunch of upper-class idiots who went to Eton. Now it's headed by a bunch of middle-class idiots who didn't go to Eton and who will implement the same policies as upper-class idiots who went to Eton.

Fluffy Mundell is the new Scotland Secretary, just as he was the old Scotland Secretary. May did want to replace him, but unfortunately Paddington Bear is busy filming a new movie. It's not like there was a whole big field to choose from, although if the new PM had just gone out into a field and chosen a lump of dead wood she'd have a Scotland Secretary every bit as useful as Fluffy.

Scotland, and most of the rest of the world, was gobsmacked by the revelation that Boris Johnson was appointed the new Foreign Secretary. Possibly this was Theresa May's way of demonstrating that she does have a sense of humour after all. We can now look forward to Boris representing the UK as he goes around the planet searching for a country that he hasn't pissed off yet.

Conservative commentators reacted to the wide-spread derision by claiming that Johnson is extremely popular throughout certain parts of southern England where lots of people vote UKIP or Tory. Or as they like to call it, the UK. It's certainly true that Boris has a degree of popularity in London. He's the city's third most popular mayor, which isn't bad going at all. Mind you there's only ever been three London mayors, but still.

It's bad enough that Boris Johnson is the international voice of the UK. Yes Scottish people, this man now represents you to foreign powers. Boris Johnson is the international face of Scotland. And if that isn't enough to make you want independence right now – in fact, yesterday – probably nothing will. Even worse than that though, is the fact that as Foreign Secretary Boris is also the head of MI6. He's James Bond's boss now, and he's licenced to shill. The head of MI6 can order all sorts of spy gadgets like ball-point pens that could blow your head off when you sign a press statement saying you're not going to back Boris's leadership campaign. Michael Gove must be pretty worried. So it's not entirely bad.

Phil Hammond is now Chancellor of the Exchequer. This is the same Philip Hammond who was defence secretary during the 2014 independence referendum campaign and came to Scotland to warn us that if we became independent we'd be defence-less against attacks from outer space. Somewhere out in the distant reaches of the galaxy there may be intelligent alien life which possesses the technology beyond our understanding that allows it to traverse the immense empty void of interstellar space, larger and emptier than the space between Fluffy's ears. As members of the UK Scotland is deeply reassured to know that this highly advanced civilisation is going to be deterred by an Astute-class submarine which failed to make a successful orbit of the Isle of Skye.

ET Phil was pronouncing on Scotland within min-utes of getting Osborne's old gig and clearing away the rolled-up tenners and bondage gear. Scotland, ET Phil said, won't get any special status that allows it to remain a part of the EU while the rest of the UK leaves. Naturally the usual suspects in the Scottish Unionist media were all over his comments, splash-ing them as a blow to Nicola Sturgeon. This wasn't really any surprise, as these are the same media outlets that the morning after Scotland has voted to become independent will carry headlines saying, Massive blow to Sturgeon as SNP loses its raison d'être.

In the real world, as opposed to the fantasy one inhabited by the more zoomy Unionists where abso-lutely everything that happens is a blow to the SNP despite the fact Scotland keeps getting closer to independence, or even the world inhabited by ET Phil's little green security threats who're going to be put off by a leaky sub, the comments were not a blow to independence at all. They were a blow to the hopes of those in the Labour Party in Scotland and the Lib Dems who are still clinging to the notion that Scotland can somehow still retain its membership of both the EU and the UK. They're going to have to face up to the truth of Scotland's situation: the only way that Scots will be able to preserve our membership of the EU is by voting for independence in a second indyref.

ET Phil's comments have just made it more likely that Scotland's not going to call the UK home.

16 July 2016

Unionists are keeping currency myths in circulation

We still don't have any confirmation on a second independence referendum, but already social media is like *Groundhog Day*: same old threats, same old dismissiveness, same old scare stories. The decision by the Scottish government to announce that it's setting plans in motion to create a Scottish currency in the event of independence were met with the predictable sulks of sneerage from the usual suspects about groats and ginger bottles.

Amongst those in whom the Cringe is strong Scotland couldn't possibly have a currency of its own. Scotland wouldn't be able to do what countries like Estonia, Latvia or Slovenia did with smaller populations, far weaker economies and far more challenging circumstances. Because Scotland, for some unspecified Unionist reasons, is uniquely incapable. Over 300 years of the Union have reduced Scotland to the status of a helpless quivering wreck that can only aspire to be a bit of a joke, and yet this is supposedly an argument for remaining within the Union that has traduced us so. Something doesn't compute.

The same people who insist that Scotland will be spending groats and ginger bottles are also insisting at the same time that we'll be forced to adopt the euro. The ginger bottle isn't a recognised subunit of the euro, but then consistency is never the top priority when a Unionist media outlet is seeking a means of denigrating Scottish independence.

The euro myth is probably one of the most persistent of all the Unionist myths about independence, despite the fact it was done to death during the last independence referendum campaign. And note how we can now talk about the last independence campaign, because now there's going to be another. The assertion that an independent Scotland would be forced to join the euro is a widespread myth up there with the myth that the Great Wall of China is visible from space (it isn't), or the myth that a goldfish has a memory of three seconds (it doesn't). These are all things that people assert simply because they've heard others assert them. They've never bothered to check. Actually a goldfish can remember things for as long as three months, which is considerably longer than most Unionist politicians can remember that their pet myths have been debunked before.

All sorts of people who really ought to know better keep repeating the myth that an independent Scotland will be forced to adopt the euro, and all sorts of media outlets who really ought to know better allow them to propagate the myth without challenging them. I'm being kind here and calling it a myth. Another, and possibly more accurate, term for it is big fat deliberate barefaced lie. Some of the people who repeat what we're kindly calling the euro myth know fine well that it's untrue.

The truth is that Scotland can't be forced to adopt the euro, and even if we did decide to adopt it, it would be several years before it became the Scottish currency. The likelihood of Scotland being forced to adopt the euro the morning after independence is even lower than the chance that Ruth Davidson will stand up in the Scottish parliament and say, "Scottish independence isn't such a bad idea after all. And you know, I don't even like tanks."

No country can be forced to adopt the euro. Despite the fevered imaginations of the Brexiteers, the EU is not a fascist unitary state bent on imposing things on member countries against their will. Members of the EU sign up to the principle that a single currency for the entire EU is a good idea, because it is a good idea, but in practical terms the EU can neither force member states to adopt it nor punish them if they don't. If an independent Scotland decides that it doesn't wish to adopt the euro, it won't adopt the euro.

Joining the euro involves a number of steps. First of all the member state needs to have its own currency, so first of all Scotland would have to establish a separate Scottish currency. Secondly the member state needs to sign up to the European Exchange Rate mechanism, ERM II, and be a member of this for at least two years. Crucially the timing and decision to do so are entirely up to the member state concerned. It's up to a member state to decide when the time is right for it to sign up to the ERM II, and it's entirely within the right of a member state to decide that the time is never right.

Other EU member states have effectively rejected joining the euro without a formal opt-out. Sweden hasn't joined the ERM II and it is vanishingly unlikely that it will do so as a referendum in the country rejected joining the euro. The attitude of Sweden is that the time is not right for it to sign up to the ERM II, and the chances are that the time will never be right. The EU can't force Sweden to join the euro, and it has no desire to force it to do so either.

The Czech Republic is also highly reluctant to join the euro. A few years ago there was a discussion in the Czech government about whether to seek a formal opt-out along the lines of the euro opt-out that the UK has. However the then former Czech prime minister Petr Nečas stated that the Czech Republic didn't need a formal opt-out as it already has an effective opt-out because it cannot be forced to sign up to the ERM II. Opinion polls in the Czech Republic show very little support for joining the eurozone.

Most of the myths about the EU rest upon stereotypes beloved by the right-wing UK media and have no basis in reality. The Brexit-supporting press would have us believe that the EU blindly applies rules and regulations irrespective of circumstances, like a glorified version of a German tourist who puts their towel on the UK's deckchair. The EU doesn't force member nations to do things that they don't want to do. It's the Westminster parliament that forces member nations of the UK to do things that they don't want to do. It's forcing Scotland out of the EU against its will. It's forcing Scotland to accept

Trident even though our elected representatives are overwhelmingly against it. So when supporters of the Westminster parliament tell Scotland that the EU will impose things on us, let's not forget who's really doing the imposing. Whether an independent Scotland ever adopts the euro will be a decision for the government of an independent Scotland, it won't be imposed by Brussels.

20 July 2016

Spanish veto of Scotland's place in EU is a Unionist fantasy

These days politics moves so quickly and turns upside down with such regularity that nowadays the most common response to a political development is, "Eh? Whit? Eh?" At least that's what it is when it doesn't actually involve swear words. In a 2 July 2016 article in *The National* I detailed some of the reasons why the much-cited Spanish veto of an independent Scotland was a myth. The past few days have seen a new turn of events which have not only provided further evidence that the Spanish Scotland veto threat is as mythical as Theresa May's commitment to governing for all the people and not just the rich, but have turned the veto threat on its head. It's not an independent Scotland seeking EU membership which has to fear a Spanish veto. It's the Westminster government and the rest of the UK seeking to leave it.

It's no secret that Spain isn't keen on movements which seek self-determination for a country or territory that are a part of another state. Spain is perhaps the closest analogue to the United Kingdom within Europe, it's made up of a collection of ancient nations – the Spanish term is "historical nationality" – which together form the Spanish state. Spain has more issues with independence movements than any other European country, even more than the UK. The fear of Catalan and Basque independence was one of the sparks for the Civil War which led to the Franco dictatorship, and many sections of Spanish society have a visceral terror of independence movements within the Spanish state in case it provokes the generals to come out of their barracks again.

But there's one issue which Spain feels far more strongly about than the fear of an independence movement in another country providing a possible example to one of Spain's own independence movements, and that's the issue of Gibraltar. Gibraltar isn't just a dry and barren rock on the south coast of Spain, it's a hugely significant site in Spanish history.

Gibraltar is a name of Arabic origin. *Jebel Tariq*, meaning Tariq's Rock, takes its name from the Arab general Tariq ibn-Ziyad who invaded Spain in 711 and founded the kingdom of Andalus which was the most advanced state in mediaeval Europe, famous for its science and learning. After the reconquista when the Muslim territories of Iberia fell once again under the control of Christian monarchs, *el Rey de Gibraltar* (the King of Gibraltar) became one of the titles of the Spanish crown, a title that the Spanish monarch holds until this day.

The UK took possession of Gibraltar when Britain involved itself in another Spanish civil war, the War of the Spanish Succession. The Spanish government feels about Gibraltar in much the same way that the UK government would feel if the site of the Battle of Hastings had become a German possession in the eighteenth century when Germany was supposedly helping one side in a British civil war. It's like inviting in a guest to help out with the rent when you're a bit short of cash, only to discover that the tenant hasn't merely stopped paying rent, they've taken ownership of your bedroom, concreted over your grandfather's prize petunias, and get regular visits from military types with nuclear weapons. Naturally Gibraltarians feel very differently about things, but the reason for this wee diversion into history is to explain the strength of Spanish feelings about the Rock.

The Brexit vote in the EU referendum has put the status of Gibraltar back in doubt again. Spain is going to be remorseless in pressing any advantage it can find in the difficult situation which the UK government has landed itself. Last week, Spanish Foreign Minister José Manuel García-Margallo threatened to veto the Brexit negotiation framework if the UK sought to include Gibraltar in the process. Spain's position is that once the UK presses the Brexit button and activates Article 50, the European Council must agree "by unanimity" to the terms of the withdrawal negotiations. The Spanish Foreign Minister believes this gives Spain the right to a veto, and he has explicitly threatened to use it as Spain will not agree to anything which recognises that Gibraltar belongs to the UK.

Also last week there was another development involving the busy Mr García-Margallo. He was interviewed on the Spanish political discussion programme *El Cascabel* (*the Rattle*) on Canal 13 TV during which he made some very interesting comments about Scotland. Funnily enough these comments have not been plastered all over the front pages of a Unionist media which gives maximum publicity to any Spanish story which puts Scotland's independence hopes in a poor light.

After speaking about Spain's difficulties with the Catalan independence movement the Foreign Minister moved on to the problems caused by the influence of extremists in European politics. He mentioned the far right candidate in the Austrian presidential elections, and then cited the malign influence of Nigel Farage and UKIP in dragging the Conservative Party and the UK out of the EU. He went on to say that as a result in his view it was likely that "within four or five years England will return to its sixteenth-century borders."

The interviewer Antonio Jiménez asked him if he was referring to Scotland, and García-Margallo confirmed that he was, adding that Scotland would seek another independence referendum in order to preserve its EU membership. Then speaking of the British Conservatives he said, "When you put the interests of your party before your country, the result is a catastrophe."

At no point did García-Margallo threaten to veto or block Scottish membership of the EU. Quite the contrary, he spoke as though Scotland's actions in seeking another independence refer-endum were perfectly understandable given the impossible situation we've been put in by the Conservatives. It would have been very easy for him to threaten an iScotland veto, given that he'd just been speaking about the actions Spain would take to frustrate Catalonia, but instead his tone was sympathetic.

So next time someone tells you that Scotland can't become a member of the EU as a result of the fall-out from the Brexit debacle because Spain would veto our membership, you can tell them that there's only one party that Spain has explicitly threatened to veto. Spain has only ever threatened to veto the Conservatives and the UK government, never to veto an independent Scotland in the EU. There's an irony you won't read about in the Unionist media.

27 July 2016

Now's the time to act as Unionists destroy the Union

Today in Glasgow there's a march and rally for independence. Just a couple of months ago Scottish independence was a distant dream, and I'd have said that it would take us years in order to slowly make the case for another referendum. Over the space of a few weeks, the Conservative and Unionist party has made a case for Scottish independence that it would have taken the independence movement years to build, and it happened without supporters of independence having to lift as much as an eyebrow. I always believed that the Union would be destroyed by the Unionists themselves, I just never expected it to happen so quickly.

A march and rally won't bring about independence, but what it will do is to send a signal, to tell those who are campaigning in their communities around the country that they are not alone, that they're part of a national movement. It puts a lie to the Unionist claim that there's no appetite in Scotland for another independence.

The same shrill voices tell us from their pettit lips that Scotland has already had its referendum. I don't recall the question on the ballot paper in 2014 being "Do you give Westminster carte blanche to do what it wants and for the Union to continue for all eternity irrespective of the circumstances?" But it seems that our Conservative government and its buffalo-riding fellow travellers in Scotland believe that's what the question said. They're wrong. Scotland's support for remaining in the Union was conditional. It rested upon the promises and commitments that those Unionist parties made in order to secure a No vote. And when Scotland voted overwhelmingly for the SNP in the Westminster general election just eight months later we put them on notice that Scotland expected them to fulfil the promises that they made to us.

That's precisely what the Unionist parties didn't do. The Tories demand that the result of the 2014 referendum is respected, but they won't respect the promises they made in order to win a No vote. The Tories demand respect from a Scotland that they refuse to respect. Scotland will not respect those who show us no respect. Respect that isn't mutual isn't respect at all. It's a demand for blind obedience.

They promised that jobs would be safe in steel-works and tax offices, and those jobs have been lost. They promised that thirteen Royal Navy ships would be built on the Clyde, then reduced the number to eight before postponing the decision indefinitely. They swore blind that the Royal Navy would never build ships abroad and now that's exactly what they're considering. They vowed to give Scotland the most powerful devolved parliament in the world, then neutered the already weak proposals of the Smith Commission while the Scotland Secretary openly boasted that the new tweaks on tax were a trap for the Scottish parliament. They promised that Scotland would be a loved and valued partner within a family of nations, and they gave us EVEL and reduced Scottish MPs to second-class status.

And then we got the biggest betrayal of all. Despite swearing blind that only a vote to remain in the UK could secure Scotland's place in the European Union, the Tories held a referendum on EU membership in order to settle their own internal party problems. And as a consequence a Scotland which voted to remain in the EU by a far larger margin than it voted to remain in the UK is to be dragged out of the EU against its will. But Scotland will be fully involved in the decision-making process, say the cold-eyed liars of Westminster. What they mean is that we might be allowed some input in deciding what colour of dog leash they'll use to drag us out.

It's bad enough that Scotland is subjected to long periods of Westminster governments that Scotland didn't vote for. There will be another general election in a few years' time. But a Brexit vote is forever. It's not just for five years. If Scotland remains in the UK, the futures of our children and grandchildren will be defined and shaped by the decisions made by Theresa May and Liam Fox and Bawjaws Johnson. Decisions we have no voice in. Decisions we have no say in. Decisions we have no control over.

This is a historic moment. Scotland stands at a junction on the path of history. We can put on the dog leash and be dragged down the path of darkness, subject to the mercies of a Westminster that treats us as a source of resources and labour to be exploited and denigrated. Or we can choose the path of self-determination, and walk towards a destiny that we define for ourselves. Those of us at the rally in Glasgow this Saturday are taking the first steps on that walk towards a future that Scotland creates for itself.

30 July 2016

No honour in a system that rewards pals and paymasters

There is famously, or infamously, no written British constitution. Instead there is a set of traditions and precedents, which is another way of saying that the British establishment makes things up to suit itself as it goes along. The British establishment is an exercise in looking after its own, and the moral bankruptcy of the entire system is summed up in the dishonourable honours system.

One well-established tradition is the right of an outgoing prime minister to bestow peerages, titles and gongs upon his personal stylist, cronies, donors and pals, and the equally well-established tradition of criticism of the awards from a morally outraged Opposition which then goes on to do exactly the same thing when it gets into power itself. As well as giving a gong to the person who helped his wife pick photogenic outfits from high street stores and allegedly advised George Osborne to get a new haircut, Cameron's list includes rewards for his aides and staff, and those who worked on and donated to his failed campaign to keep Britain in the EU.

Cameron came into office claiming that he wanted to clean up politics, but all he's done is to tarnish it even more than it already was, which to be fair is quite a remarkable achievement. If the currency of democracy is the shiny coin of public trust, the British penny is caked in rust and decayed to its heart. The honours system is, in theory, a means of rewarding people who have made a substantial and notable contribution to public life, but during his time in office, Cameron has given peerages to at least thirteen people whose sole contribution and service to public life is that they gave a large amount of money to the Tory Party. He's given knighthoods and gongs to many more.

New Prime Minister Theresa May has announced that she's not going to interfere with Davie passing out rewards to his pals because, as a spokesapologist for her office said, "It would set a very bad precedent." Which is another way of saying that she doesn't want any future PM to interfere with her crony list when it's her turn to reward her personal stylist, the person who grooms the resident cat, her party donors, and the people who scratched her back on her climb up the political greasy pole. The only Number 10 insider who doesn't benefit from an outgoing prime minister's honours list is the cat itself.

We've been here before of course. Ten years ago Tony Blair's government was enmeshed in a scandal after Blair tried to bestow peerages on a number of individuals whose sole contribution to public life appeared to be that they'd given the Labour Party large loans at very favourable rates of interest. The SNP's Angus MacNeil and Plaid Cymru's Elfyn Llwyd made an official complaint alleging that the law prohibiting the sale of honours had been breached. During the resultant investigation the prime minister was interviewed three times by the police. Although no charges were laid, the entire episode contributed to the perception that British politics were out of touch, self-serving and a means for the British establishment to reward itself at the expense of the people. The perception has become established that British politics is an exercise in cronyism – a perception which has only become more deeply entrenched as time has gone by.

At the time David Cameron was the leader of the Opposition, and speaking about the scandal said, "We've got to stop this perception that parties can somehow be bought by big donations either from very rich people, or trade unions, or businesses." And here we are, ten years down the line, and Davie is contributing to that very same perception. He's done this before of course: just a few months ago he awarded a peerage to the controversial Lynton Crosby, the Australian strategist who came up with the tactic of demonising Scottish influence on the British government which won Cameron his majority.

Labour isn't any better. Recently the former director of the human rights charity Liberty Shami Chakrabarti was asked whether she'd been offered a peerage by Jeremy Corbyn after she carried out the Labour Party's internal review into ant-Semitism. She refused to answer, sparking off speculation that she had indeed been offered a place in the Lords. Ms Chakrabarti has at least made more of a contribution to public life than a party donor, but the impression given was that peerages are being doled out in return for services rendered to a political party.

The honours system is inseperable from the parliament of patronage that is the House of Lords. The UK has a second chamber stuffed full of unelected representatives who owe their ermine bedecked places to party favours, backscratching and cronyism. Despite the fact that it's been Labour Party policy to abolish the Lords ever since the Labour Party was founded, over one hundred years later the undemocratic institution remains as undemocratic as ever. Tony Blair assumed power in 1997 promising to reform the insitution, which was then full of elected peers as well as appointed life peers, and managed to replace it with something even worse. He abolished the right of most hereditary peers to sit in the Lords, and stuffed it full of even more placepersons that he appointed himself. His successors have only continued the discredited tradition.

No political party in Britain is going to reform the honours system into something that is actually honourable. Having a system of patronage in place is far too useful. It allows parties to reward their donors and their pals, and it allows politicians a secure retirement home from which they can continue to benefit from the public purse and exert political influence over our laws without any of that troublesome business of standing for election. If the Labour Party didn't do anything about the honours system and the House of Lords which is fed by it when they had a crushing majority in the Commons, you can be quite sure that they're never going to. The only people who will defend the honours system are those who've already benefitted from it, or who hope to in the future.

3 August 2016

Newsflash — a *Scottish Six* on its own is no longer enough

This week there was new life breathed into the aged proposals for an hour-long *Scottish Six* news programme to replace the *BBC News at Six* and *Reporting Scotland*. Although it was first mooted almost twenty years ago, Scotland is still no nearer to a decent publicly owned national broadcast news service worthy of the name. For all that the Unionist parties and Westminster insist that Scotland is the devolviest country in the devolved history of devolviness, we're not even a parish cooncil as far as broadcasting is concerned.

Where Catalonia has its own twenty-four-hour news channel, Scotland has to make do with half an hour of murrdurrs, cute fluffy kittens and the fitba after the proper news informing us about the rest of the planet and non-parochial matters like the state of schools in Berkshire and the success or otherwise of the English cricket team. Other people's parochialism is BBC Scotland being cosmopolitan.

Scottish news provision is in the news again because a committee consisting of non-Scottish MPs and a single SNP representative unanimously voted to support the idea of a separate Scottish news programme. It wasn't because the BBC management spontaneously decided after almost twenty years to notice that devolution has occurred and to do something about it. In fact Scotland's influence within the BBC is decreasing as a result of recent reforms to the structures of the corporation, just as the money devoted to Scottish programming is also decreasing. The director of BBC Scotland has been effectively demoted, and instead of being a member of the top tier of BBC management will now report to a "director of regions and nations".

The BBC prefers to remain in a 1980s fantasy Britain where devolution hasn't happened, where the prospect of Scottish independence remains the preserve of beardy men in kilts who take to the hills on a weekend to re-enact mediaeval battles, and where we're all a big happy Great British family that regards London as the centre of the universe. As all the other public institutions and corporations that were publicly owned were broken up and sold off by the Conservatives and a Labour Party which aped them, the BBC, the armed services, the monarchy and the Westminster parliament itself are the only British institutions that are left.

As Britishness has receded in other spheres of life, the BBC has become more hysterical in its attempts to promote a dying sense of nationhood. The most inconsequential competitions get Great British prefixed to their titles as though there was something quintessentially British about baked goods products or sewing which is alien to the rest of the world. In the Great British flag-waving world of the BBC, no one in France sews couture, and no one in the Black

Forest bakes gateaux. We get wall-to-wall coverage of the most inane event in the lives of the overprivileged royals, to the accompaniment of professional sycophants who gush over our TV screens like stalkers at a Lady Gaga concert. We get all of this, in the name of non-parochialism, but we don't get a decent Scottish news service, because that would be trivial.

A *Scottish Six* news programme is to be welcomed in the same way that getting to the end of the Strand is welcome progress on a journey from Trafalgar Square to Scotland. But unless there is serious devolution within the BBC, what we're likely to see is a glorified version of *Reporting Scotland* or the risible *Scotland 2016*, a politics show that was so inept that even political junkies wouldn't watch it. There are blogs with a larger readership than there were viewers of the supposedly flagship politics show of BBC Scotland.

Twenty years ago a *Scottish Six* news programme would have been cheered. Today it's too little too late. Scotland has moved on. What we need isn't a Scottish news programme: we need a Scottish national broadcaster. There is no justification whatsoever for refusing Scotland what every other self-governing nation has, a public service broadcaster that allows citizens to keep informed about the issues that face them. Yet the Unionist parties resist this tooth and nail, claiming that it would be controlled by the SNP while they deny that the BBC is controlled by them.

The simple fact is that if the Unionist parties sincerely believed that the BBC is not controlled or influenced by Westminster and its priorities, then they would have no worries about a Scottish broadcaster being controlled by Holyrood. By refusing to countenance a Scottish broadcaster, they only fuel the suspicions of independence supporters that the BBC is biased against Scottish independence. They say that they don't want a Scottish broadcaster which produces pro-independence propaganda because we've already got a British broadcaster that produces Unionist propaganda. Because if the BBC was genuinely independent and neutral then it would be beyond the wit of our politicians to devise a structure for a Scottish broadcaster that would ensure its neutrality too.

So let's welcome a *Scottish Six*, but it's just a tiny step towards what Scotland really needs, a Scottish-based public service broadcast service. A *Scottish Six* is Scotland receiving a few crumbs from the Great British restaurant of the BBC, but we need a restaurant of our own.

6 August 2016

GERS figures take the biscuit for bringing nothing to the indy debate

This week has seen the annual Unionist Fest, celebrated with unseemly glee by the Tories and those parties that don't want another referendum unless it's an EU one. It's the *Great British GERS Bake Off*, cooking the books since the 1990s. The annual GERS sponge was started by Governor General Ian Lang, the Mel Giedroyc of the Conservatives only without the winning smile, the charm or the mass appeal. Or indeed any appeal at all, which is why his party decided that what it really needed in order to head off the constant demands for Scottish self-government was a set of annual figures showing that Scotland was a bit of an economic basket case.

Well I say a bit. What the UK government would have us believe is that uniquely amongst the nations of north-west Europe, a country with almost all the UK's oil, most of its fish, more energy resources than the Duracell bunny on speed, whisky, tourism, and a whole load of other advantages that Greece would give both the arms of the Venus de Milo for, is in fact more indebted than a shopaholic with a platinum credit card. And even more, they want us to believe that it's entirely our own fault, and not the fault of the parliament that's determined Scotland's economy for the past 300 years. Thankfully they are assisted in this by a press that's more supine than a limbo dancer without a vertebra, otherwise known as the Scottish Conservative and Unionist Party.

In Toryland, the only arguments are economic arguments, bereft as they are of anything that could be described as a principle. The political case for independence is unanswerable, so the only way to stifle Scottish voices calling for the radical principle that a country might just be best governed by people who actually live in it, or have a government that is accountable to Scottish voters, was to come up with a set of figures showing that Scotland makes Greece look like Switzerland when it comes to financial probity. And so GERS was born, the bastard offspring of an accountant on smack and a *Daily Express* editorial.

GERS has succeeded wonderfully in depicting Scotland as the Burkina Faso of northern Europe. Even when the oil price was higher than a Russian athlete's urine sample, every release of the GERS figures somehow managed to prove that Scotland was utterly dependent on the good graces of the Westminster parliament and its love of charitable handouts to small Celtic nations. Every release of the figures is accompanied by the ritual smugging of Unionist politicians whose ProudScottery depends upon proving that Scotland couldn't possibly manage a European level of public services without wads of Bank of England banknotes being tossed across the border for grateful Scots to collect like snottery weans picking up coins at a wedding scramble.

Although the GERS figures began life as a Unionist tool to batter down the argument for Scottish self-government, they've failed miserably to do so. Independence supporters merely point out that if indeed the GERS figures prove that uniquely amongst the countries of northern Europe Scotland is financially incapable, despite the country's immense advantages, then that's the fault of a Westminster parliament which has had its paws firmly on all the levers of macroeconomic control for the past 300 years.

Even worse for the Unionist cause however, GERS has succeeded too well in another respect. The figures may have convinced some in Scotland that our country is reliant upon English handouts, but they've also convinced many more English people that Scotland only enjoys its public services courtesy of the English taxpayer. And having withdrawn from the European Union because they were not happy with subsidising feckless European nations, they're not entirely enthralled with the notion of subsidising what they see as a feckless Scotland either.

The GERS figures never succeed in making anyone change their mind. Independence supporters are convinced that they're a big pauchle and hide the truth that Scotland is really a perfectly normal northern European nation; Unionists are equally convinced that they demonstrate that Scotland is special. Because as well as wanting us to believe that Scotland is uniquely the economic basket case of northern Europe, despite being the richest part of the UK outwith the south-east of England, the

Unionists also want us to believe that Scotland is the beneficiary of the largesse of a parliament that has never been noted for its charity. If we are to take the GERS figures at face value, then all by themselves they are a demonstration that the UK is broken and that the Westminster parliament has no interest in fixing it.

All the GERS figures really do is to reinforce existing positions and breed resentment on both sides of the Tweed. They change no minds, they add nothing of value to the argument about Scotland's future. The reality of GERS is that they tell us as much about the finances of an independent Scotland as they do about who's going to win the new season of *Bake Off*.

27 August 2016

UK will be the loser in this assault on our human rights

While the British media obsessed over seating arrangements on a train that the unelectable Jeremy Corbyn was taking to a debate with the equally unelectable Owen Wossisname as they contested leadership of the unelectable Labour Party, the Tories were quietly getting on with the serious business of sticking a knife in the back of what's left of British social democracy and overcrowding Westminster with their own supporters.

It was confirmed last week by UK Injustice Secretary Liz Truss that the Tories are to press ahead with the abolition of the Human Rights Act. The Conservatives want to replace it with a human rights act that's more British, which presumably means redefining human as "a member of the British establishment". Everyone else will be treated like cattle, just as they already are on Britain's overcrowded railways. Actually it's worse than that because cattle get a free ride, but the only ones on the most expensive rail network in Europe who get a free ride are the train operators.

Theresa May has ordered a review of the plans. The human rights plans that is, she doesn't propose to do anything about Britain's lucidrous railways which charge you more for a ticket from Glasgow to

Birmingham than it costs to fly to somewhere you might actually want to visit. Theresa doesn't think that the original plan to abolish the Human Rights Act was snooperish enough because it conceded that human rights laws in the UK would remain subject to the European Court of Human Rights. Theresa doesn't want anything to get in the way of her right to read your emails so she can find out where you're flying to instead of standing in a corridor on an over-priced privatised train to Birmingham.

The Tories aren't noted for their concerns for civil liberties. Neither are former Home Secretaries like Theresa May. Every new appointee to the post of Home Secretary ends up being described as the most authoritarian Home Secretary ever, and Theresa was no exception. She's now been succeeded in the post of Most Authoritarian Home Secretary Ever by Amber Rudd, who's going to be responsible along with Liz Truss for abolishing what's left of our human rights.

The claim is made that the Human Rights Act needs to be abolished because it prevents the UK from deporting foreign criminals. But that's not true. Foreign criminals can be deported, it's just that they can't be deported to countries where they're going to be tortured or executed, which is perfectly reasonable because the UK doesn't allow prisoners to be executed or tortured, much as certain right-wing newspapers would like them to be.

So what the abolition of the Human Rights Act will achieve is the deportation of foreign criminals to countries where they can be tortured. That's not really a goal that's worthy enough to destroy the human rights protections of UK citizens, but getting rid of foreign criminals was always only an excuse. The real reason the Tories want to abolish the Human Rights Act is that they can't countenance anything that blocks the train corridor between them and absolute power and control, especially when what's standing between them and their fetish of parliamentary sovereignty has European in its title.

Theresa May's British Bill of Rights isn't about human rights at all, because there's no logical reason why the human rights of a British human need to be any different from the human rights of any other human. What Theresa's British Bill of Rights is really about is the absolute power and sovereignty of the Westminster parliament. It's the Westminster Bill of Rights, and the only humans whose rights have primacy are those who are in charge in the Westminster parliament. That would be Theresa and her pals.

Instead of enforcing an internationally recognised standard of human rights, the Tories are going to give us their own version of British rights. You'll have the right to watch *Strictly*. You'll have the right to vote for the *X Factor*. You'll have the right to put up bunting when some minor royal marries another posh person. You'll have the right to stand on a crowded train. You'll have the right to work for a pittance in a low-paid job. You'll have the right to trudge through the rain to a food bank after your benefits have been sanctioned. What you won't have is the legal right to take any complaints to a forum which isn't controlled by the Westminster parliament or those it appoints, because the right of Theresa May to tell you what to do is greater than any right you might imagine you might have to mount a legal challenge to her. That's what a British Bill of Rights means. We might be called British citizens these days, but we're still subjects.

Human rights legislation is enshrined in the Scotland Act. The Human Rights Act is part of the foundation of the Scottish parliament along with the European Convention on Human Rights. According to the Sewel Convention, the Westminster government can only make changes to the Scotland Act with the agreement of the Scottish parliament. The Scottish government has already said that it's not going to give consent. If the Tories want to strip UK citizens of their human rights and replace them with the right to do as the Tories tell us, they can do so without Scotland's cooperation. That means that the only way in which Theresa May can abolish the Human Rights Act is to ignore the Sewel Convention and impose it on an unwilling Holyrood. So much for treating Scotland as a respected and valued partner in a family of nations.

We live in a state where much of the media is more concerned about whether the number of seats on Jeremy Corbyn's train proves that he's a loser than it is about a government that's whittling away the basic human rights of British citizens. Meanwhile there's another train coming down the line that they're all oblivious to, a Scotland that's on the tracks to independence. When it collides with a British state hell-bent on stripping Scots of their human rights protection, the only loser is going to be the UK.

31 August 2016

Scotland would be listened to, consulted, respected? Not then and not now

It seems so long ago now, back in those frantic days of the fag end of the referendum campaign, when the Better Together campaign was making promises of better behaviour like a forty-a-day smoker with a hacking cough and looming hospital appointment. Scotland was going to be loved. We'd be listened to, we'd be consulted, we'd be respected. We were going to have a valued leading place within the most perfect family of nations in the history of the multiverse, a family so ideal that we'd go on *Dr Phil* to give everyone else lessons in interpersonal relationships.

Even before the Unionist commentators on the referendum results show had time to perfect their smug grins, Scotland was rammed firmly back into the cereal box and we discovered that Westminster's condition was still smoking forty a day and blowing the smoke in our face. But we are being respected, no really. Scotland is being respected by Westminster in the same way that a mugger respects his victims by not actually spitting in their faces and confining his abuse to the verbal.

With each and every promise made by the Unionist parties during the independence campaign having gone the same way as Gordie Broon's reputation for statesmanship, Scotland was promised that we'd at least be consulted during the Brexit process and would be fully involved in negotiations. That promise has now gone the same way as all the others. This week the prime minister made it clear that her government and it alone would decide the terms of Brexit and when and how negotiations on Article 50 would begin. Scotland will get what it's given. Or more accurately, Scotland will put up with whatever it is that Westminster decides to take away from us.

The Tories respect Scotland so much that the Scottish Secretary, the so-called voice of Scotland in the Tory cabinet who's really the voice of the Tory cabinet in Scotland, wasn't even at the meeting. His presence was not required so he was away in hiding because his government has decided to break another promise to Scotland and close down military bases in Inverness and Moray. He's just the message boy whose job is to tell Scotland what his bosses have decided is in store for us. Fluffy Mundell could be replaced by a stuffed toy and no one would notice. In fact, it's quite likely that he already has been.

The respect we're being shown is a bit like being told that even though you didn't want to go and see the new Adam Sandler movie, and let's face it who does, and even though you wanted ice cream and not popcorn, you'd at least be allowed to decide what sort of popcorn you wanted. You're being consulted, so shut up and stop complaining. Only now you discover that even though you asked for sticky toffee flavour, you're going to get the stale unsalted and unsweetened variety, the kind that makes polystyrene packing chips seem tasty. Now eat up your popcorn, watch the movie and make like you're enjoying yourself. Isn't it great being better together?

Theresa May's government looks like it's going for a so-called hard Brexit, the worst of all possible worlds as far as Scotland is concerned. The Tories fondly imagine that all they need to do is stamp Theresa's ruby slippers and the EU will magically give them full access to the single market while simultaneously allowing the UK to block the free movement of people. It's British exceptionalism at its worst, the attitude that Britain is a special little flower and normal rules of international cooperation don't apply. But the other EU countries have a very different idea, and they're the ones who have a much stronger hand to play in any negotiations. They have a vested interest in discouraging any other country from leaving the EU, and that means they're not going to be inclined to do the UK any favours.

The UK government has as its priority the need to block further immigration, but Scotland needs more immigration in order to grow its population. After decades of deindustrialisation, thanks to decades of Westminster economic mismanagement Scotland has been left with historically high levels of emigration and an ageing population. That in turn means that Scotland has a higher expenditure on social welfare and health care because it's disproportionately the elderly and those with health issues who remain. That all feeds into the budget deficit that the Unionists keep crowing about as a reason for

Scotland not being able to finance itself as an independent state. Yet those same Unionists are denying Scotland the means to do anything about it.

Within a UK with a block on immigration, Scotland's population is only going to age even more – a process which is exacerbated as our young people leave to seek work down south while older people from the rest of the UK see Scotland as an ideal retirement home. Our future in the UK is going to be as a care home, and expenditure on health and social welfare is only going to increase even more with fewer and fewer active young people contributing to the economy.

Meanwhile we will have lost our rights as European citizens, lost the European subsidies to our farming industry and development funds to deprived areas, and we'll be an isolated impoverished corner of a xenophobic and isolationist Britain. That's the respect that Westminster has in store for us, a respect that deprives Scotland of its self-respect. It's time we did something about it and voted to decide our future for ourselves. It's time we stood proud.

3 September 2016

Scotland isn't asking May for her permission on indyref2

In an interview with Andrew Marr on the BBC on Sunday, Prime Minister Theresa May poured out a big bowl of Brexit cereal and insisted that Scotland eat it up, without any milk or sugar. Our unelected Tory PM doesn't think that there's any reason for Scotland to have a second independence referendum. Scotland wasn't the only region of the UK to vote to remain, she said, consigning the historic nation of Scotland, a constituent nation of the UK, to the same status as Lambeth.

It's not a question of could Scotland have a referendum, opined Theresa, it's a question of should, making it very plain that in her opinion Scotland has as much justification for having another referendum as a dalmatian does of advising Cruella De Vil on coat designs.

In May's view, Scotland voted to remain a part of the UK in 2014 and in 2016 the UK voted to leave the EU and the spotty little Scots will do what the rest of the UK tells them to. Forget that the Better Together campaign that she supported spent much of 2014 banging on that the only way Scotland could ensure its EU membership was to vote No. In fact in March 2014 she asserted that a Yes vote in that year's independence referendum would see Scotland being forced out of the EU, with the clear inference that the only way Scotland could remain an EU member was for us to vote No. Now she's quite happy to see Scotland forced out of the EU. It's amazing how much a mind can change in two years. That's our unelected PM for you, the Oh Dear Leader of the UK.

Theresa is allowed to change her mind, but Scotland isn't. Even though we were told by Theresa herself that we could only remain a member of the EU if we voted to stay a part of the UK, she doesn't think that Scotland has any right to reconsider its position now that Theresa has reconsidered her own position. In the UK, changing your mind is the prerogative of Tory politicians; everyone else gets to do what they tell us. At least that's what Fluffy Mundell thinks his job description is. No one in Scotland has spoken to the Tories for years, they don't like to be interrupted.

No wonder so many in Scotland suffer from the Cringe. It doesn't matter how we vote or what we say we want, we get Fluffy Mundell as a voice of authority. It's hardly surprising that the only way to reconcile being Scottish within the UK is to have lower self-esteem than someone whose ex-partner was a hoarder, and who then realised that they were the one thing that their ex was able to dump.

The UK that Scotland voted to remain a part of in September 2014 doesn't exist. The UK in which Scotland was a loved and respected partner in a family of nations was shown to be a fantasy within a couple of hours of the referendum vote being announced.

There is no faster safer devolution. There is no job security for tax office workers or shipbuilders. There is no Scotland that leads and whose voice is heard in the corridors of power. And now there's no European Union membership either. There are *Doctor Who* plotlines which are more firmly grounded in reality than the promises made to Scotland by the Unionists during the independence referendum campaign. Scotland has every right to reconsider its position when the UK government and the Unionist parties altered their own position as soon as they secured the voting outcome that they wanted.

The question is not should Scotland have another independence referendum. It's not even could Scotland have another independence referendum. The only real question is when Scotland has it. And there's an easy answer to that question. Scotland is going to have another independence referendum when the independence campaign is going to win it. That's a whole lot sooner than Theresa might think. As soon as she presses the big red Brexit button, the countdown to a second independence referendum starts.

The time to have another independence referendum is after the UK government has officially notified the EU that it's activating Article 50, but before negotiations are concluded. That means that a Yes vote in indyref 2 will allow Scotland a smooth transition into the EU in its own right, without having to leave. The Unionist parties and the usual suspects claim that Brexit has had no effect on the desire for independence and that opinion polls haven't moved, but there's no reason to expect any polling movement because Brexit hasn't happened yet and the independence movement hasn't started its campaign of persuasion. Once the economic ill effects of the UK's departure from the EU start to become clear, once the grassroots indy movement gets going, the polls will begin to move in favour of independence.

Theresa May can tell us there shouldn't be another independence referendum until she's bluer in the face than is usual for a Tory, but the campaign has already started. What the Tories don't seem to realise is that ordinary Scots don't require the permission or approval of the Conservative Party before embarking on an independence campaign. If we needed their permission before we got constitutional change we'd still not have a parliament and the government would be telling us that *Reporting Scotland* was dangerously separatist.

All over Scotland local groups and organisations are getting back together, are organising themselves, and developing strategies and campaigns which will lead Scotland to independence in a revived and revitalised movement. We're rebuilding a grassroots movement, energising and enthusing activists and campaigners, and building a head of steam that will lead to an unstoppable demand for a second referendum. We're campaigning in the most politically active and aware country in Europe, and this time we're starting from a much higher base.

The independence movement is not a creature of a political party. This is not Nicola Sturgeon's independence campaign. All of us, ordinary Scottish people, we're doing it for ourselves. We're the only people who count in this campaign. Theresa May might claim that Scotland shouldn't have another independence referendum, but the Scottish independence movement isn't asking her permission or opinion.

7 September 2016